POPULAR SNOWSHOE TRAILS

OF THE

Canadian Rockies

ANDREW NUGARA

RMB

For information on purchasing bulk quantities of this book, or to obtain media excerpts or invite the author to speak at an event, please visit rmbooks.com and select the "Contact" tab.

RMB | Rocky Mountain Books Ltd.
rmbooks.com
@rmbooks
facebook.com/rmbooks

Cataloguing data available from Library and Archives Canada
ISBN 9781771604352 (paperback)
ISBN 9781771604369 (electronic)

All photographs are by the author unless otherwise noted.

Printed and bound in China

We would like to also take this opportunity to acknowledge the traditional territories upon which we live and work. In Calgary, Alberta, we acknowledge the Niitsitapi (Blackfoot) and the people of the Treaty 7 region in Southern Alberta, which includes the Siksika, the Piikuni, the Kainai, the Tsuut'ina and the Stoney Nakoda First Nations, including Chiniki, Bearpaw, and Wesley First Nations. The City of Calgary is also home to Métis Nation of Alberta, Region III. In Victoria, British Columbia, we acknowledge the traditional territories of the Lkwungen (Esquimalt, and Songhees), Malahat, Pacheedaht, Scia'new, T'Sou-ke and W̱SÁNEĆ (Pauquachin, Tsartlip, Tsawout, Tseycum) peoples.

We acknowledge the financial support of the Government of Canada through the Canada Book Fund and the Canada Council for the Arts, and of the province of British Columbia through the British Columbia Arts Council and the Book Publishing Tax Credit.

Disclaimer
The actions described in this book may be considered inherently dangerous activities. Individuals undertake these activities at their own risk. The information put forth in this guide has been collected from a variety of sources and is not guaranteed to be completely accurate or reliable. Many conditions and some information may change owing to weather and numerous other factors beyond the control of the authors and publishers. Individuals or groups must determine the risks, use their own judgment, and take full responsibility for their actions. Do not depend on any information found in this book for your own personal safety. Your safety depends on your own good judgment based on your skills, education, and experience.
It is up to the users of this guidebook to acquire the necessary skills for safe experiences and to exercise caution in potentially hazardous areas. The authors and publishers of this guide accept no responsibility for your actions or the results that occur from another's actions, choices, or judgments. If you have any doubt as to your safety or your ability to attempt anything described in this guidebook, do not attempt it.

Contents

Stunning Wapta Falls. (Shawn Benbow)

Introduction

The Canadian Rockies in winter are nothing short of spectacular. Endless kilometres of untouched pristine terrain, strikingly beautiful mountains everywhere the eye can see and snow and ice scenery that is guaranteed to render you breathless. Regardless of how many visits to the mountains you have made in the summer, you really haven't experienced the Rockies until you have seen them up close during the snow season. There is absolutely no place I'd rather be on a crisp, cold and clear January day than in the Rockies, surrounded by mountains and snow, a deep blue sky above and the sun illuminating the landscape in unequalled brilliance.

Getting around the mountains in winter has unique challenges. Many choose to negotiate the landscape on cross-country or AT (alpine touring) skis, others simply go on foot, while a few more take the motorized approach on a snowmobile. Then there are snowshoes.

Snowshoeing is fun, great exercise and allows you to travel into places of surreal beauty that would otherwise be inaccessible during the winter and spring. The activity is growing in popularity at a phenomenal rate in western Canada.

This book was written for people who are just getting into snowshoeing and want to start with easy trips. All the routes in the book steer clear of avalanche terrain and most require only a reasonable level of physical fitness. As well, young children can complete many of the trips in this book. Most of the official snowshoe trails are included in this guidebook.

Before a beginning snowshoer "aims for the skies," a healthy dose of easy and hazard-free trips are compulsory. Hopefully, this guidebook offers just that. When all is said and done, many snowshoers will decide that the easy trips in this book and similar trips are all the adventure they require, and that is just fine!

The Preliminaries

Before setting out to enjoy some of the most wondrous scenery on this planet, it is important to be properly informed about snowshoes, snowshoeing and the environment you will be entering. Ignorance is not bliss here – it can be deadly! Please read all the preliminary information presented in the next section before setting out.

The Changing Face of Snowshoeing

The world of snowshoeing seems to be undergoing rapid changes and shifts in focus. Historically, snowshoeing was a primarily utilitarian activity – that is, snowshoes provided an efficient means to get from A to B when the terrain between A and B was covered in deep snow. The invention of backcountry skis and significant design improvements over the past 35 years, however, have dramatically decreased a person's need, and often his or her desire, to use snowshoes for practical travel in the backcountry. Thus, snowshoeing has started to become more recreational in nature.

Although snowshoeing as a recreational activity can be traced back to the late 19th century, it is in the mid- to late 20th century that we have seen a significant increase in this pastime. Fifty or so years ago, the recreational aspect of snowshoeing may have been limited to following summer trails or exploring open areas of low-angled terrain – basically, easy hiking in the winter. However, with the recent and tremendous increase in the number of people taking to snowshoes, and significant technological advances in snowshoe design, snowshoers can now set their sights on far loftier objectives that formerly were the domain of mountaineers and ski mountaineers.

Do Snowshoes Really Work?

I'll let the following photos by Dave McMurray and Nicole Lisafeld answer that question!

Of course this is not always the case. Postholing while wearing snowshoes is not completely uncommon, especially early in the season. However, as a general rule, snowshoes will dramatically improve your flotation, eliminating most nightmares. Also, snowshoes prevent the brutal shin-bashing ordeals that many encounter when they break through a hard layer of snow (much like the crust of bread) only to have their shins bash into that layer. It can be quite painful!

The Benefits and Advantages of Snowshoeing

Snowshoeing is great for your health and easy on your wallet, and practically anyone can do it. In addition, snowshoes can take you to places inaccessible to you when you are on skis or foot. Provided you approach the activity sensibly, you have everything to gain by exploring the mountain environment on snowshoes.

Health

The health benefits of snowshoeing are undeniable and profound. Snowshoeing is as good a physical workout as you can get in the winter. Calgary's Fit Frog Adventures (www.fitfrog.ca) considers snowshoeing to be a safe, cross-training, conditioning sport that provides simultaneously a low-impact, aerobic, strength-training and muscle-endurance workout. As an aerobic workout, snowshoeing will help you improve or maintain cardiovascular fitness. As well, because snowshoeing uses every major muscle group at relatively high intensity for extended periods of time, it requires high caloric expenditure (400–1000 calories per hour).

ABOVE: *The author unsuccessfully tests out life without snowshoes. Lindsay Rousseau clearly knows better! (Nicole Lisafeld)*

RIGHT: *Jeff Lang courageously perseveres through some extreme postholing on Mount Backus. Note the depth of the snowshoe tracks in front. (Dave McMurray)*

Further, choosing snowshoeing as your primary winter-training activity has many benefits. Fit Frog notes that if you are a runner, substituting snowshoeing for running during the winter may improve your running fitness more than simply running through the winter. The muscles snowshoers use are the same ones used in walking and hiking hilly terrain. However, snowshoers' hip flexors may receive more of a workout and their quadriceps may get more exercise than walkers' or hikers' would; this is because of the lifting motion of each snowshoeing step. As well, snowshoeing on slopes works not only the hip flexors but also the extensors, which are important muscles for cyclists. Finally, if you choose to use poles while snowshoeing, your shoulders, arms and back muscles will also get a workout!

Expense

Snowshoeing is also a very inexpensive form of winter recreation. Assuming you already have the appropriate footwear (hiking boots), the only equipment needed is a pair of snowshoes ($100–$300) and a set of ski or hiking poles ($50–$150). That's quite a deal compared to the average $1,200–$2,000 price tag for a decent AT setup (skis, bindings, skins, boots and poles). Renting snowshoes is also incredibly inexpensive – as low as $10 a day. For those who are new to snowshoeing and unsure if they will take to the pastime on a regular basis, renting is a great idea.

Who Can Snowshoe?

Anyone can snowshoe! Although a cliché, the saying "if you can walk, you can snowshoe" is fairly accurate. Those of us who have been walking for many years already have a huge head start in gleaning snowshoeing skills compared to those learning how to backcountry ski! Unlike backcountry skiing, the learning curve for snowshoeing slopes gently. While for some it may take a trip or two to become completely comfortable on snowshoes, many will learn the art within hours of stepping out into the snow. Essentially, snowshoes just make your feet bigger – quite a bit bigger – so, if you can walk with really big feet, you can snowshoe.

Of course, the "anyone can snowshoe" rule does not apply to the extreme end of snowshoeing – snowshoe mountaineering. The technical demands of that activity require formal training and are outside the scope of this book.

"To Boldly Go Where No One Has Gone Before"

The only significant advantage snowshoeing has over backcountry skiing is superior manoeuvrability in tight spaces. This applies specifically to treed terrain. Weaving in and out of closely spaced trees on skis can be a nightmare – not so on snowshoes. There are some areas and peaks that are accessible in the winter only on snowshoes.

A secondary advantage to snowshoeing over skiing is the footwear required. Anyone who has scrambled or climbed wearing ski mountaineering boots knows how awkward they can be. Snowshoes allow you to choose footwear appropriate to the terrain you may encounter. Hiking boots are sufficient footwear for all trips in this book.

Another small advantage snowshoes have over skis is that they are less susceptible to damage when on rocky terrain. Naturally, it is strongly recommended that you remove your snowshoes when snow has given way to rock, or if there are unavoidable rocks protruding from the snow. However, if these rocky sections are short-lived, the effort of taking your snowshoes off and then putting them back on minutes later may not be worth it. Stepping carefully should be enough to avoid any damage to your shoes.

Types of Snowshoeing

Since there are three types of snowshoes, most sources divide snowshoeing into three categories – racing, recreational and mountaineering. The focus of this book is the most basic form of recreational snowshoeing: snowshoeing that doesn't take you into avalanche terrain and requires no formal training in the fundamentals of mountaineering.

Types of Snowshoes and Buying Equipment

Snowshoes have evolved considerably since the early days of wooden frames bound together with animal-hide webbing. Today's snowshoes are lightweight, extremely durable and easy to put on and take off. They have superior traction and can be used to ascend steep slopes that would have been impossible with older-style snowshoes. The types of snowshoes available are categorized according to the types of snowshoeing described above. For example, racing snowshoes are small and light. They are designed to allow you to run in your natural stride. Racing snowshoes are not appropriate for trips in this book.

As snowshoe design has advanced, in

The lightweight Atlas Rendezvous.

The Tubbs Flex TRK. The traction rails, just visible at the left, are an excellent feature of this snowshoe.

The Tubbs Flex VRT offer superb ease of use and superior performance.

recent years the differences between recreational snowshoes and mountaineering snowshoes have become less and less distinct. Your average pair of recreational snowshoes now has good crampons for better traction, heel lifts for steep slopes and advanced binding systems to keep the shoes firmly attached to your feet. I have one pair of mountaineering snowshoes and two pairs of recreational snowshoes. I routinely take the recreational ones on more serious terrain and have never found them lacking.

Having said that, most companies are still (and for good reason) producing snowshoes for three different uses:

- Trail-walking snowshoes are designed for flat or gently rolling terrain. Usually these models do not have heel lifts and have toe and heel crampons only. If you intend to go only on well-used trails with little to no steep terrain, these snowshoes will serve you well. As of 2016, specific models include Tubbs Flex ESC, Roam and Meridian; Atlas Rendezvous; and MSR Evo and Revo Trail.

- Hiking snowshoes are designed for steeper terrain and off-trail travel. Most models have heel lifts and aggressive crampons. These snowshoes can provide a good compromise between the other two categories and will be more than enough snowshoe for all the trips in this book. If you are interested in leaving the beaten path and tackling steeper terrain, these are the recommended type to use. Specific models include Tubbs Flex TRK, RDG, Elevate and Xpedition; Atlas Access and Treeline; and MSR Revo Explore and Lightning Explore.

- Mountaineering snowshoes are designed for serious backcountry travel involving very steep terrain. This is more snowshoe than you will need for any trip in this book, but there are only minor differences between mountaineering and hiking snowshoes. If at some point you intend to transition to intermediate and advanced snowshoeing, you will eventually want to use mountaineering snowshoes. Specific models include Tubbs Flex Alp, VRT, Mountaineer and Xpedition; Atlas 12 Series and Aspect; and MSR Revo Ascent and Lightning Ascent.

I presently have three pairs of snowshoes that all see their fair share of use: the Atlas 11 Series, the Tubbs Flex TRK and MSR Lightning Ascent. My MSR Lightning Ascent snowshoes come out for serious mountaineering ascents. The entire frame of the Lightning acts as a crampon, and it gives unparalleled traction on steep terrain.

For easier trips and terrain, I use the Atlas 11 Series. They offer excellent flotation and traction and a solid binding system that effectively distributes pressure over a maximum area of the foot (Wrapp Plus bindings). This snowshoe is built with an aluminum V frame that also has a durable stainless steel toe crampon and flexible decking. The heel strap adjusts easily.

For more serious trips where I may encounter steeper and potentially icy terrain, I go with the Tubbs Flex TRK. The traction rails on these snowshoes are fantastic,

offering amazing grip and stability on hard-packed and icy surfaces. In addition, this snowshoe has the Flex tail and torsion deck, which also aids in stability. Wearing these shoes, I've ascended 30° icy slopes with ease. The simple but effective binding system is also excellent.

My newest and most aggressive pair of snowshoes is the Tubbs Flex VRT and they are fantastic! The DynamicFit binding, featuring the Boa Closure System, produces evenly distributed tension around your boot and the Viper 2.0 toe crampons dig deep in any conditions. These shoes are super easy to put on and take off, and of course the traction rails give superb grip on the iciest and steepest slopes. For any trip that I consider "serious" the Flex VRT are on my feet!

If you plan to undertake trips in this book, I recommend that you look into a hiking snowshoe model. As stated, they are well suited to most types of terrain and give you the option to be a little adventurous if the spirit moves you. After all, life does often take you into places where you never thought you would go (just don't venture into avalanche terrain).

Snowshoe Sizes

After you have determined what type of snowshoe you are going to use, getting an appropriate size becomes the issue. Adult snowshoes now come in a wide variety of sizes, ranging from 21 to 36 inches. The width of most modern snowshoes varies from 8 to 10 inches.

The balance a good snowshoe must strike between flotation, weight and manoeuvrability can be a delicate one. Larger snowshoes have better flotation, but they are heavier and less manoeuvrable in tight places. Smaller shoes offer good manoeuvrability but less flotation. On long trips with extensive sections of trail-breaking, the reduced weight of smaller-sized snowshoes will be negated by the increased difficulty of breaking trail. Renting various sizes of

Wearing my Baffin boots with snowshoes on a very cold day in January.

snowshoes and trying them out can be a good strategy for determining what size works best for you, before committing to the purchase of a specific size.

For more objective guidelines, the specific size you choose is determined primarily by your weight and what type of terrain you plan on tackling. For your weight, as a general guideline we can designate 22 inches as being small, 25 inches as medium, 30 inches as large and 36 inches as extra-large. Use the following very basic parameters as weight guidelines. The weights include your clothes, boots, backpack and additional equipment.

• Under 32 kilograms – kids
• 32 to 59 kilograms – 22 inches
• 59 to 77 kilograms – 25 inches
• 77 to 100 kilograms – 30 inches
• Over 100 kilograms – 36 inches

In regards to terrain, if you intend to snowshoe only on well-packed trails and rarely engage in deep trail-breaking, you can also afford to get a smaller-sized snowshoe, since flotation will not be of great concern. Those snowshoers who want to get out into the deep stuff will want to choose a larger size.

When choosing a pair of snowshoes, going to a reputable snowshoe dealer and asking for advice is always a good idea.

Footwear

Buying appropriate footwear for snowshoes is an easier activity than buying snowshoes because snowshoers most frequently use regular hiking boots. Be sure to treat your boots with a water-resistant barrier before heading out. Since the average air temperature you'll experience on most snowshoeing trips is considerably lower than it would be on the same trip during summer, keeping your feet warm is paramount. Buying hiking boots that are a half-size or even a full size too big is often an effective strategy for dealing with cooler temperatures. The extra space in the boots allows you to wear two or even three pairs of socks if necessary. For temperatures ranging from −5°C to −20°C, I will often wear a thin pair of liner socks and one or sometimes two pairs of thick wool socks. This combination always keeps my feet warm, and I have never developed blisters or suffered other foot irritations. Make sure your socks aren't too tight. Tight socks constrict blood flow to your feet and soon lead to cold feet.

When the temperature drops below −20°C, hiking boots may not be enough to keep your feet warm. In this case, footwear designed specifically for colder temperatures may be necessary. Baffin makes boots that are rated to −50°C. Should the temperature ever plummet to those kinds of levels, personally I have no intention of stepping out of the house, let alone traipsing around the mountains. However, it is comforting to know that if you do, your feet will be well protected. The weakness of these boots is that they are often too big to take crampons. As such, you may be limited to trips of a less serious nature.

Additional Equipment

The intermediate to advanced snowshoer may need to pack crampons, an ice axe, climbing gear and other paraphernalia to complete a trip (and make your pack really heavy). Fortunately, for the beginner snowshoer there is no need to worry about such things. The only piece of additional equipment needed is a set of poles.

Poles

Ski poles or trekking (hiking) poles with baskets are essential for all snowshoers. Even on "very easy" flat terrain, poles have their purpose. Primarily, poles are used for stability, balance and support: they turn a biped into a quadruped. As such, poles can reduce strain and stress on your knees, ankles and feet. In the same way that fallen skiers use their poles for leverage to regain a standing position, so too can snowshoers use a similar technique, though it is not as difficult.

As a general rule your arms should form a 90° angle when holding the poles in front of you. The length of your poles will need to be different when going up- or downhill – shorter for uphill and longer for downhill.

Although having poles is essential, it's your choice whether to use them or not, much the same way as one can choose to wear snowshoes or go on foot. On beginner trails that don't involve trail-breaking and/or steep sections, poles may be of little use. Having said that, I would never leave them in my car. On easy trails, I attach my trekking poles to my backpack and take them out when needed. Ascending steeper terrain without poles is usually not too difficult. Descending that same terrain can often be much easier with poles. They can be used for balance and also enable you to lean forward a little when descending, thus helping you to keep your weight over your feet. Another reason to bring your poles and have them handy is to clean off snow, which can ball up on the bottom of your snowshoes.

All of this said, poles are not essential for young children, whose low centre of gravity can make poles more of a hindrance than a help.

For adults, however, a collapsible set of poles is strongly recommended, for their ease of use, adjustability and for carrying them on your pack.

Clothing

Clothing doesn't really qualify as additional equipment, unless of course you usually go out naked, but this is a good place to talk about the specific kinds of clothing you will need when snowshoeing.

Dressing in layers is the key to being comfortable outside in the winter months. Wool and synthetic materials, such as polypropylene, work best. Most people wear a base layer, a mid- or insulation layer and a waterproof yet breathable outer layer.

When travelling outdoors in the cold

ABOVE: *With Mount Outram in the background, Mark and Dan demonstrate their flawless technique!*

BELOW: *Poles used for balance and stability on steeper terrain.*

months, you can never take too much extra clothing with you. Though impractical to take a spare of everything, your backpack should at least have one or two pairs of extra socks, an extra top layer and extra gloves. A balaclava or equivalent is also essential. When preparing for a trip, I often ask myself: Will the contents of my pack allow me to survive should I be forced to bivy overnight?

When considering clothing, it is also important to remember that even if the forecast calls for a warm, windless day, conditions can deteriorate very quickly and without warning. You must be prepared for anything. The clothing contents of my backpack are usually the same whether the forecast low is –5°C or –30°C.

Also note that high and low temperatures in weather forecasts are for the valley bottoms. Expect the temperature on a summit to be significantly colder than what has been predicted for the valley. A windy summit can exacerbate already low temperatures to an alarming degree.

When travelling in cold temperatures, it is important to minimize sweating or completely avoid it if possible. Ironically, sweat caused by generating body heat can lead to hypothermia when you slow down or stop. The sweat cools very rapidly and can cause your body temperature to do the same. Stopping and taking the time to remove or add layers of clothing when necessary is one of the keys to safe winter travel.

Sunscreen and Sunglasses

Finally, don't forget to pack a tube of sunscreen with a high SPF (I use a 60) and a good pair of sunglasses that have 100 per cent UV protection. The sun's rays reflecting off snow can be intense. Getting a serious sunburn or burning the corneas of your eyes happens more easily than you might think.

Other Winter Traction Devices

A good pair of snowshoes will provide excellent traction on any snow and/or ice surface. However, if the terrain is more a combination of ice and bare ground or ice throughout, then a different form of traction is in order. Having another form of traction has almost become a necessity these days, especially for front range trips, where snow conditions can vary wildly from week to week.

Kahtoola Microspikes. Great traction and they fit any boots or runners. Awesome purchase!

Tony Daffern has written a terrific article on the other types of winter traction devices, on his and Gillean's kananaskisblog.com. Personally (and Tony agrees), I have found Kahtoola Microspikes to be best suited to the types of terrain you may encounter in the Canadian Rockies. Microspikes are very well designed and rugged and provide excellent traction, digging into ice or hard-packed snow with ease. They are a little heavier than other traction devices, but that extra weight is necessary for good performance and durability. You will find Microspikes referenced multiple times throughout this book. If I suspect at all that I may need them at any time during a trip, Microspikes are in my backpack.

The Snowshoeing Season

Snowshoeing season in the Canadian Rockies usually starts in December and ends in mid-May. The earliest snow of the season, in October and November, is often not consolidated enough to make snowshoeing worthwhile. Of course, unconsolidated snow can persist during any month of the

You need to be prepared. An hour before my icicle eyebrows formed, the sky was clear and the temperature quite mild.

season; it all depends on the prevailing weather. Objectives in the Front Ranges, where the snow may not be as deep, can provide decent day trips during these months. However, they may not be snowshoe trips. Be prepared to carry your snowshoes on your backpack for long stretches.

That said, the Rockies' snowpack in December and into January is typically a tough one to snowshoe on. Powdery, unconsolidated snow offers little to no support, even for snowshoes. This may cause you to experience the unpleasant phenomenon known as postholing, where you sink through much, if not all, of the snowpack. As such, expect trail-breaking during this time to be physically taxing. Again, the Front Ranges may be your best bet. Also, objectives along Highway 742 will start to see some traffic at this time of the year, and you may even find a fully broken trail!

Late January and February often see the snowpack gain strength as the melt–freeze cycle runs its course. By late February, hopefully, you will experience a significant decrease in the postholing ordeals that are so common in December and January. Reduced hours of daylight will limit you to shorter routes, but that should not pose a problem for trips in this book. Also note that these, along with March, are the best months to snowshoe on lakes. The ice and snow surface on most lakes is very strong during these months.

March and April are generally the best snowshoeing months. The snowpack at this time is usually strong and supportive, daylight hours are a little longer, temperatures are milder (although above treeline you can still expect to encounter brutally cold conditions) and trails have already been broken and reinforced. Plan to try some longer trips in these months. By April you will probably be looking at objectives farther west, as warm spring weather will often put an abrupt stop to snowshoeing in the Front Ranges. The warmer temperatures associated with daytime heating also mean you have to be more aware of afternoon avalanches.

Important Note: Many of the routes described in this book that involve snowshoeing on or around lakes will become less feasible by mid-April. Realistically, many lakes may still have another solid month of strong ice, but personally I always start to err on the side of caution around mid-April when thinking about lake trips. Refer to the section "Frozen Lakes" on page 27 for more information.

May can also be an excellent month for snowshoeing, but forget about going on lakes. All lake routes in this book will be off limits unless you plan to snowshoe around them, not on them. Areas near the Continental Divide are often still under a substantial layer of snow. Head up the Icefields Parkway and visit Bow Lake (but stay off the lake) and the Peyto Lake Viewpoint. Isothermal snow could be your greatest nemesis on May trips. This condition occurs after repeated melt–freeze cycles, which cause the temperature of the whole snowpack to be consistent (0°C), thereby making the snow weak and unsupportive. As well, snow that is supportive in the morning can be soft and slushy in the afternoon. At this time of year, even if your snowshoes end up on your backpack instead of your feet, it's still a good idea to take them along and hope for decent snow.

You are really pushing the season if you pack your snowshoes when you head out to the Rockies in June. Still, it is possible in certain years and certain areas to find snowshoeing conditions in late spring. Expect your snowshoes to spend most of the trip affixed to your backpack. Areas farther west, such as Lake Louise and Yoho, may be your best bets. Clearly, unless you want to use your snowshoes as flippers for swimming, don't go anywhere near a lake in June.

Snowshoes or No Shoes?

The question whether to wear snowshoes or go on foot arises often in snowshoeing. This is especially true in low-snow years, when chinook winds have melted the snowpack, very early or very late in the season, or for trips to the Front Ranges. As a very general rule, I would recommend that you should wear snowshoes if the snow is of any depth greater than 5 centimetres. Snowshoes help your balance and allow you to take big, aggressive, confident strides without the fear of stepping into a snow-covered hole and breaking your ankle. Wearing my snowshoes, I have run down snow-covered slopes that I would not have dared to run down on foot, in fear of falling or tripping and breaking some body part!

The added traction that snowshoes offer, even when the snow is not deep, is a tremendous benefit. This is especially noticeable on hard-packed snow and icy terrain. Many people will choose to carry their snowshoes when they find themselves on trails, such as Chester Lake, that have been fully packed down. I would say that this is actually one of the best times to put your snowshoes on. Heavy traffic on any trail will eventually cause icy and slippery sections to develop. Your snowshoes will help you to negotiate this kind of terrain with ease. Although I can recall, with some degree of embarrassment, several face-plants into the snow, when my snowshoeing technique became careless, I cannot remember a single incident of slipping with snowshoes on. I have slipped many times on snow and ice when wearing hiking boots.

If the snowpack is shallow, it may be easier to ascend on foot and then descend wearing snowshoes. This strategy gives you more freedom to move fast and can be very effective on uneven terrain. For this reason, if my snowshoes are not on my feet, they are attached to my backpack. On countless ascents, I've trudged up a mountain on foot and then enjoyed a speedy descent on snowshoes. You may regret leaving your snowshoes behind, but rarely will you regret carrying them, even if they stay on your pack throughout. At an average weight of 1.9 kilograms, snowshoes are a relatively light addition to your backpack.

All of this said, however, travelling on foot to the detriment of an established trail is always bad form. Postholing creates holes that may be dangerous to other snowshoers and skiers. You should wear your snowshoes if there is a chance you might damage the trail.

The aesthetic experience of gliding and fluid movement is one of the joys of backcountry skiing. While snowshoeing has no such equivalent, over the years I have come to appreciate the beauty and freedom of movement with snowshoes. While not as pronounced as carving perfect turns with skis, plunge-stepping rapidly down a steep snowy slope on snowshoes can be very exhilarating and the rhythm of moving through deep snow is its own aesthetic. Just another reason to place the snowshoes where they belong (for the most part) – on your feet!

When all is said and done, the decision to use snowshoes or go on foot is an individual one. I would say as a final personal note that if you intend to go snowshoeing, SNOWSHOE!

Snowshoeing with the Family

For those looking for an outdoor winter activity for the whole family, snowshoeing can't be beat. As stated, snowshoeing is easy and inexpensive, certainly a cheaper alternative to a day at a ski resort.

Children as young as 3 are usually capable of strapping on a pair of kids' snowshoes and making strides through the snow. Most snowshoe companies make models specifically for the different weight categories of children. The smallest size of snowshoes are designed for children 3 to 5 years old and up to 19 kilograms. These snowshoes weigh only 0.7 kilograms.

If you have young children with you, very short trips on well-packed trails are recommended. Remember that children may have to take two or even three steps to your one. Obviously, the older the child, the longer the route you can take on. Children 10 and up are usually ready to tackle some fairly long trips and as an added bonus are also ready to break trail for you!

Although they may not be able to snowshoe, children younger than 3 can still accompany you on a day out in the Rockies. Regardless of the manner in which you bring young ones along – listed below – I strongly recommend that you stick to easy, relatively flat and well-travelled routes. The sometimes uncertain nature of trail-breaking may put a child in danger should you fall or step into a tree well, creek or other hazard.

- Pull toddlers along in a Chariot Carrier with the CTS Cross-Country Ski Kit. The Chariot offers more protection than a baby carrier and will not affect your balance as much. As well, the Chariot is very comfortable for the child, allowing for longer trips. The child may even take a nap! The Chariot works best on the easier routes, such as Cameron Lake (see *A Beginner's Guide to Snowshoeing in the Canadian Rockies*). It glides easily across the snow and performs well on routes with very gently graded terrain. More challenging and steeper terrain like Chester Lake can be done with a Chariot, but such routes will prove to be more challenging for you because of the push and pull of the Chariot. (A second person walking behind the Chariot to help guide it does help on routes like Chester Lake.) I do not recommend using the Chariot on routes with tight curves because of its large turning radius. Please note that you must use the five-point harness in the Chariot to ensure the safety of your child.
- Carry children aged 3 and under in

Kids, snow and snowshoes – a recipe for fun and good times. (Anita Hofer)

baby carriers specifically designed for the outdoors. Baby carriers are just like backpacks and allow you to tackle steeper terrain and narrower trails without compromising manoeuvrability. Be sure to research specific models and choose a high-quality carrier. That does not necessarily equate to a high price. Mountain Equipment Co-op (MEC) makes a very inexpensive carrier (the Happytrails Child Carrier backpack) that does its job wonderfully.

- Pull toddlers along in a toboggan or sled. This method is very inexpensive, but toboggans are also often cumbersome and difficult to manoeuvre. If you choose to use a sled, pick very short, easy trips that cover flat terrain.

One note about taking the kids out: don't expect them to stay clean or dry. Kids will be kids, and they may have more fun trying to swim in the snow than snowshoe across its surface. Pack some dry clothes for them to change into when you get back to your vehicle.

Trip Ratings

The trip ratings in this book are not equivalent to those found in *Snowshoeing in the Canadian Rockies*. Even though there are beginner routes in that guidebook, it is geared toward intermediate and advanced snowshoers, who are used to multiple hours of strenuous trail-breaking, steep terrain up to 35°, avalanche assessment and the basics of mountaineering. Since all routes and areas in this guidebook stay away from avalanche terrain and require no formal training in mountaineering techniques, the three rating levels correspond primarily to trip length, trail-breaking challenges, general steepness and the amount of elevation gain required.

Descriptors for each rating are as follows:

- **Easy** – A trip on flat or very gently graded terrain. Completion times from 0.5–3 hours and elevation gains less than 100 metres. Strenuous trail-breaking is unlikely, though there may be some trail-breaking after a snowfall.
- **Intermediate** – Sections of steeper

ABOVE: *The Chariot Carrier, with the CTS Cross-Country Ski Kit.*

BELOW: *The Chariot in action on Cameron Lake (see* A Beginner's Guide to Snowshoeing in the Canadian Rockies*).*

terrain but still manageable. Completion times from 2–4 hours and elevation gains from 100–300 metres. Possibility of some strenuous trail-breaking.

- **Advanced** – Short sections of steep terrain up to 25°. Completion times of 3–6 hours and elevation gains of 300+ metres. Strenuous trail-breaking is

likely. Snowshoes with good crampons are recommended.

These are just general guidelines, of course, and some trips don't fit all the criteria of each rating. For example, Chester Lake requires only 310 metres of elevation gain but is rated Advanced because of several short, but steep, sections. Similarly, the Ink Pots

Mark, Rogan and the MEC Happytrails Child Carrier.

earn an Intermediate rating (even though the trip breaks the mark of 300 metres of elevation gain) because the terrain is moderately graded.

Avalanches

With a few minor exceptions, there are no routes in this guidebook that go into avalanche terrain. As such, it is not necessary for users to carry avalanche equipment or

know how to use it. However, even a beginner snowshoer may want to leave the beaten path and go exploring, simply for the enjoyment and reward of the activity itself. Therefore, the following section on recognizing avalanche terrain is included in this book. If you do venture away from the described routes, being able to identify potential avalanche terrain will give you

ABOVE: *Michael enjoys the snow in the best way possible! (Ken Schmaltz)*

BELOW: *The Nugara clan at Crandell Lake. Sixteen-month-old Rogan took the Chariot there but insisted on exploring the lake on foot.*

the ability to stop and go back immediately. Unless you have taken an avalanche safety training course (AST 1 and/or AST 2), and are carrying avalanche equipment and know how to use it, do not tempt fate by continuing. Every year backcountry users are injured or killed by avalanches. Statistically, most avalanche incidents involving humans turn out to be fatal.

Regardless of whether you intend to go into avalanche terrain or avoid it completely, it is a good idea to become acquainted with the avalanche bulletins at www.avalanche.ca. These bulletins give an up-to-date and comprehensive analysis of present avalanche conditions.

The excerpt below is taken from *Snowshoeing in the Canadian Rockies* and is intended for snowshoe mountaineers; however, it is every bit as applicable to those who seek only to avoid avalanche terrain.

Recognizing Avalanche Terrain

Gaining the ability to recognize avalanche terrain is the first step in the complex process everyone must go through to ensure safe travel in winter. With proper training, lots of reading and a diligent effort in the backcountry, the following skills can be learned and developed quickly.

Slope Angle

The most important factor in determining if terrain has the potential to produce an avalanche is slope angle: angles between 25° and 60° have that potential. Generally, angles of 35° to 40° produce the largest number of slab avalanches. Slopes of these angles deserve the most scrutiny and should be carefully studied and tested before traversing or ascending them.

Measuring the angle of a particular slope is best accomplished using an inclinometer. Use of this tool is especially important when you are first developing avalanche-recognition skills. Putting a specific number to your own observations will dramatically increase your ability to accurately determine a slope angle without an inclinometer.

Always be aware that in regards to "eyeing" the angle of a particular slope, human perception has limitations. Often what appears to be low-angled can be far steeper than estimated and vice versa; this is something to think about when heading to that 20° slope that is actually 38°.

Slope Orientation

The leeward slope is the side of the mountain that is opposite to the direction from which the wind is blowing. As such it is usually wind-loaded and very unstable. In the Canadian Rockies, the primary wind direction is from west to east and southwest to northeast. Therefore, slopes facing east or northeast are far more likely to be avalanche-prone than those facing west and southwest. Remember that this is just a generalization and by no means infers that all west- and southwest-facing slopes are safe. Serious destructive avalanches occur on all slopes.

Slope Shape

Three terms describe slope shape: convex, concave and planar (see diagram below). Avalanches can occur on all three types; however, convex slopes present the most serious risk for a slide. The shape of a convex slope puts a great deal of stress on the snow just below the bulge. Always be on the lookout for convex slopes and be ready to assess possible consequences if they release.

Concave slopes, because of their bowl-like shape, are capable of supporting the weight of the snow above them to a greater degree than convex or planar slopes. This rule only applies to a certain extent, however. When that weight becomes excessive, concave slopes will release, just like convex ones do. The location from which an avalanche may start on a concave slope is difficult to determine.

The consistent angle of planar slopes means they can avalanche anywhere.

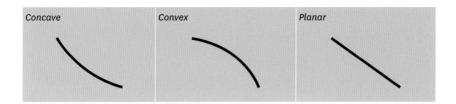

Concave   *Convex*   *Planar*

Anchors

As the word implies, anchors help keep snow attached to the slope it's on, thus rendering the slope more stable than one without anchors. Anchors include trees, vegetation and rocks. Unfortunately, like many other aspects of avalanche physics, anchoring is a double-edged sword. The snowpack around anchors is obviously thinner and therefore weaker and prone to instability. In other words, avalanches can start around anchors.

Forested terrain on a slope is typically a good indicator that the slope is relatively safe. When a slope is abundantly covered in full-grown trees, you know there has usually been little to no avalanche activity on that slope for a number of years. Ascending through heavily treed terrain is always preferable to being out on open steep slopes.

Elevation

The categories of terrain and their corresponding ratings on the avalanche bulletin provide pretty clear evidence that the higher you go the more avalanche risk there is. On rare occasions the ratings may be the same in each zone, but the overwhelming majority of days will see a more severe rating for terrain in the alpine than below it. Increased elevation means more snow and more wind to blow that snow around. As a general rule, as soon as you move above

Mount Joffre displays the three types of slopes. C=concave, V=convex, P=planar.

ABOVE: *A cornice on Red Ridge.*

BELOW: *A large overhanging cornice on Kent Ridge North.*

ABOVE: *The deep-blue sky that often accompanies a high-pressure system. Of course the sun must be in the right position. Taken from Commonwealth Ridge, with Chester Lake just visible near the lower right.*

RIGHT: *A shapely cornice and low-lying clouds on an ascent of Kent Ridge Outlier.*

treeline and into the alpine, expect the avalanche risk to rise.

In conclusion, hopefully the preceding text will at least introduce you to the very basics of recognizing avalanche terrain. I would encourage all winter mountain users to take an avalanche safety course regardless of your goals. You simply can't be over-informed about the subject. If you can recognize avalanche terrain, you can stay away from it.

Other Hazards and Considerations

While of primary concern, avalanches are certainly not the only elements of nature to be cognizant of when out on snowshoes. Cornices, glaciers and bad weather can be just as deadly.

Cornices

Cornices are one of my favourite aspects of winter travel. These shapely and unique formations can add tremendously to the scenery and views on any trip. However, they can also be a source of great danger. Having a cornice collapse beneath you will probably have deadly consequences. As it may be difficult to ascertain whether there is solid rock beneath the snow you are travelling on, it is always best to play it safe by staying very far away from the edge when snowshoeing or hiking along a ridge. Cornices can grow to enormous sizes and may

On an ascent of Whirlpool Ridge, low-lying clouds blanket the valley below.

overhang the edge of a ridge by a signifi-cant distance.

Cornices can be dangerous not only when you are near them. When cornices collapse onto steep slopes they can trigger massive avalanches. The cornices hanging off the summit ridge of Mount Ogden are classic examples (see Sherbrooke Lake, page 153).

Although cornice danger is fairly limited in the routes described in this guidebook, it is certainly something to be aware of.

Bad Weather

Inclement weather can be troublesome at any time of the year, but the trouble it causes is especially pronounced in the winter months. Getting caught in a snow-storm with whiteout conditions can be very serious. A storm will quickly cover up the tracks you made, making it difficult to re-trace your steps. This is not likely to be too big of a concern with beginner routes, but if you do choose to go out when the weather

is suspect, pick the shortest and easiest routes where route-finding is very straight-forward. Better yet, refer to the section en-titled Picking Good Weather Days (below), and try to avoid nasty weather completely.

Limited Daylight

On December 21 of each year, the mountain parks receive a little less than 8 hours of daylight. That's not a large number when compared to the 16.5 hours we get on June 21. Plan your day accordingly and always have a headlamp with extra batteries in your backpack. A forced bivouac in winter is not only unsavoury because of the cold temperatures but also because you may have as much as 16 hours of darkness to get through.

Standard time (November–March) also means that early starts are almost impera-tive. Thankfully, the daylight situation dramatically improves after the second Saturday in March, when clocks in Alberta move ahead an hour for daylight saving time. This doesn't impact the amount of daylight hours available but at least puts the sunset an hour later, allowing for longer trips or later starts.

Picking Good Weather Days

Snowshoeing is very much a good-weather activity. Lacking the exhilarating run down that skiers are accustomed to, or the speed of a snowmobile, the primary thrill of snowshoeing comes from experiencing beautiful surroundings. Clear skies enhance that experience to an infinite degree.

Predicting the weather in the Canadian Rockies is often a crapshoot at best. Many meteorological factors contribute to the uncertainty of weather forecasting in this area, factors that render even the most experienced and knowledgeable forecasters incapable of accurate prediction of the weather. In short, be prepared for any type of weather and be understanding when the weather is not as glorious as one of the local forecasters predicted. Of course, many times I've gone to the mountains, a bad weather forecast in hand, only to enjoy beautifully clear skies.

Following are some procedures to go through and some tips for maximizing the amount of time you spend under clear skies and minimizing that spent under clouds.

Check the weather forecasts online. Environment Canada, Accuweather and The Weather Network are presently the most popular online sources for weather in Canada. Monitor the forecasts several days before your trip, but expect them to change frequently. Always check again the night before your trip and, if possible, the morning of the trip.

Look at a current satellite image just before the trip. Sometimes the satellite image very much contradicts the forecast. In general, I trust a satellite image far more than a computer-generated forecast. Knowing how to read and analyze weather patterns from satellite images can be a very useful skill and may save you from spending a frustrating day in bad weather.

High-pressure systems are your best friend. When the forecaster on the local news mentions "a ridge of high pressure," start salivating and do your best to get out to the mountains. High-pressure systems are generally predictable, stable and result in the best possible weather.

Be flexible about changing your plans at the last minute. Bad weather in one area of the Rockies does not mean bad weather throughout. In general, the farther west and the farther north you go, the worse the weather. The Front Ranges may be basking in full sunshine while mountains of the Continental Divide are consumed by clouds.

All of the above doesn't mean you should stay at home on cloudy days. Sometimes cloud cover can lead to very atmospheric lighting and views. Also, on very rare occasions, the clouds may be lying very low in the valley, and you can ascend above them, which is always an amazing experience.

Frozen Lakes

Snowshoeing routes on or around frozen lakes, streams or rivers make up almost 40 per cent of the trips in this book. Therefore it's very important to know some facts about them, especially the lakes. The best time to go out onto a frozen lake is between mid-December and April. However, an unseasonably warm autumn or spring might encroach on that time span, and discretion and caution should be used. In 2002, for example, a late-December sojourn out onto Emerald Lake ended abruptly when the ice started cracking beneath me and a friend. Thankfully we were very near the shore at the time and got off the ice before I became Leonardo DiCaprio (Jack Dawson) slowly sinking into the unfathomable depths. January, February and March are almost guaranteed to be safe for lake traverses.

A lake's elevation is an important factor in determining how soon into the season it

The beautiful and varied terrain of Spray Lake. Mount Shark is to the left and Mount Turner the right.

freezes. At a low elevation of approximately 1400 metres, Barrier Lake (not described in this book) may not be safe for travel until January or even later. In contrast, Spray Lake (see page 68), sitting at an elevation above 1800 metres, can be frozen to a depth of over a metre by mid-December. Keep this in mind if you are planning to take an early-season excursion onto a frozen lake.

If you are wondering about how much weight the ice on a frozen lake can handle, on a March attempt of Mount Nestor, my brother and I witnessed a full-sized truck drive the entire length of Spray Lake, right down the middle. Admittedly, we instantly felt a little foolish about the apprehension we experienced when crossing the lake with snowshoes, several hours earlier. Needless to say, this example cannot be applied to all frozen lakes. Spray Lake does have a notable reputation for thick ice. However, I wouldn't be risking my brand-new truck on Barrier Lake during any month – good thing I drive a Honda CR-V!

An actual determination of the strength of the ice you will be travelling on in the Canadian Rockies is almost always an impractical proposition, simply because the ice will most likely be covered in deep snow. Excavating the snow to get a look at the ice is hardly worth the time and energy. Also, if you have to dig through a significant amount of snow to get to the ice, this usually indicates the ice will be quite strong. The best way to be confident of ice strength is to simply go to the mountains in January, February and early March.

Nevertheless, there are several points you should be aware of:

- Ice at an inlet or outlet to a lake can be very weak, even if the ice on the lake is very strong.
- The strongest ice is blue to clear in colour; the weakest will be light grey to black.
- A slushy ice surface is a warning that the ice is weak and/or deteriorating below.

- Ice thickness of 10 centimetres and greater is suitable for snowshoeing.

The south end of Spray Lake is my favourite of the lake trips, boasting terrific views of the surrounding mountains and interesting ice, which you can see when it is blown clear of snow. The great thing about Spray Lake is that you are afforded completely different views and perspectives from either end or from the middle of the lake. Other lakes that you simply must visit (preferably on clear days) are Emerald Lake (page 156), Sherbrooke Lake (page 153), Bow Lake (page 165) and Waterfowl Lakes (page 171).

Snowshoeing Technique

You would think that snowshoeing requires little, if any, technique. After all, it's simply walking with bigger feet. Certainly snowshoeing does not require all the skill and technique that accomplished backcountry skiers possess, but there are some techniques that make snowshoeing an efficient, safe and enjoyable experience. Most of the techniques described in the subsections Getting Up, Getting Down, and Side-sloping (below) are for more advanced snowshoers, but even beginners should be aware

of them, just in case they find themselves on difficult terrain.

Flat Terrain

There are really no great revelations to be made relative to snowshoeing on flat terrain. You simply walk with as normal a stride as the width of your snowshoes will permit. The narrow design of most modern snowshoes makes this very easy. Although you may have to widen your gait slightly, you will very quickly adapt to it. Soon, you won't even be aware you are taking a wider-than-normal step.

Getting Up

Following are some different techniques you may wish to employ on steeper terrain, as well as some useful tips to keep in mind.

1. If your snowshoes have heel lifts, put them up to reduce strain on your calf muscles and Achilles tendon.
2. Snowshoe in switchback patterns so you are not going directly up a steep slope.
3. If the snow on steeper slopes is soft, kick-step into it with your snowshoes, then flatten the snow by stepping down into it.

LEFT: *Going straight up a relatively gentle slope.*

RIGHT: *Using a herringbone technique on the same slope higher up.*

ABOVE: *Descending a steep slope by facing in and kick-stepping.*

BELOW: *Running downhill on snowshoes can be fast and fun. Michelle and Nicole race down a small hill on the way back from Burstall Lakes.*

4. If the snow is hard, use snowshoes with aggressive crampons. The best styles are advanced models that allow the frame of the snowshoe to act as a crampon. When using this type of snowshoe, maximize the amount of the frame making contact with the hard snow surface. Frame crampon snowshoes can tackle slopes up to a very steep 35°.

5. For steeper slopes of soft snow, a similar technique to the skiing herringbone (feet angled out) may work better than switchbacking (see photos).

Traversing a steep slope of hard snow – heel lifts turned up, snowshoes pointing forward.

Getting Down

Like ascending, descending gentle slopes on snowshoes is very easy. Plunge-stepping and even running downhill can be fun and will get you down in no time at all. Steeper slopes require more attention to technique. When going downhill, keep the following tips in mind:

1. Bend your knees slightly and keep your weight over your feet. Avoid the temptation to lean too far forward. Use poles for balance and support.
2. For steeper slopes, it may be necessary to face into the slope and descend using a kick-stepping technique. Your poles can be used for balance and also in a self-belay technique, similar to that used with an ice axe.

Side-sloping

When side-sloping (traversing) go slightly uphill as you go across.

1. In soft snow, kick-step into the slope with the inside edge of your snowshoe.
2. In hard snow, use the snowshoes' crampons. Traversing very steep slopes may require you to face into the slope and move sideways, keeping your snowshoes pointed uphill. This technique allows for the most effective use of the snowshoes' crampons.

Running

If you do decide to run wearing recreational snowshoes, remember to lift your knees higher when running through powder – the deeper the snow, the higher the lift. You don't need a pair of racing snowshoes to run, but recreational snowshoes will be more difficult and clumsy to run in. Go slowly at first and get used to the feel of moving fast. Also note that running is best done without poles.

For those looking for some rigorous cardiovascular and muscular exercise, running in snowshoes provides an intense workout.

Balling

Balling is the accumulation of large and often heavy clumps of snow on the bottom of your snowshoes. This occurs when warm temperatures have softened the snow. Balling makes travel very difficult, and you have to stop often to clear away the snow from the snowshoes. Unfortunately, very little can be done to prevent it, although I have heard that spraying your snowshoes' crampons with non-stick cooking oil can help. Having a set of ski or trekking poles to knock away the snow is the best way to deal with balled-up snow. Sometimes just banging the side of your snowshoe with a pole will release the snow; other times you have to dig it away.

Another method that sometimes works quite effectively is to flick your heel violently as you step. This causes your snowshoe to bang up against your heel, knocking away unwanted snow.

Snowshoes with large crampons are more prone to balling.

Trail-Breaking

Breaking new trail on snowshoes can be all things: fun, tiring, exhilarating, challenging or a physical brutality of Biblical proportions! You may experience one, two or all of the above when wading through new snow. Here are a few things to keep in mind:

1. Try to keep a consistent stride and make your stride shorter for deeper snow.
2. Lift your knees high.
3. Pace yourself. You don't want to expend all your energy and then give up (or not have enough energy to return).
4. Go in a group (a large one if possible) and take turns breaking trail.
5. Put the person with the biggest snowshoes at the front of the line (sucks to be big!).
6. Walk in single file to pack down a solid trail that will be easy to return on.

Keep those knees high. Michelle and Nicole run through fairly deep powder.

Try to keep a positive attitude when trail-breaking becomes arduous. Remember that you are forging a path that will then be infinitely easier to return on. This is especially true when you are going uphill. I vividly recall a solid 90 minutes of brutally strenuous, uphill trail-breaking going up to Smuts Pass in December of 2009. I recall with even greater clarity the exhilarating 18 minutes of plunge-stepping to get down that same slope on return.

When all else fails, I try to stick in my head the old proverb, "The journey of a thousand miles begins with the first step." Even if you are moving farther away from your vehicle, every step you take is one step closer to it. That rationale has helped me get through some pretty long and exhausting days in the mountains.

A group of 17 breaks trail through deep snow in Kananaskis, off Highway 742. (Bernie Nemeth)

Snowshoeing Etiquette

As more and more people make their way into the mountains on snowshoes, good etiquette becomes increasingly important. There really isn't much to snowshoeing etiquette, but in following and respecting a few basic guidelines we can ensure a good relationship with all mountain users, such as skiers, hikers and snowmobilers.

Ski Tracks and Trail-Breaking

The most important guideline for snowshoers is to avoid snowshoeing on ski tracks whenever possible. Many winter trails are wide enough to support separate tracks for skiers and snowshoers. If a ski trail has already been established on the route you are on, make a new trail for snowshoers as far away from the ski trail as possible. This may seem like a great deal of effort when an established trail is right there, but trail-breaking is the price of travel for all winter users. At some point, everyone must take on the burden of breaking new trail. If all travellers share that responsibility, then it is possible that you may only have to break new trail a few times each season. Everyone who follows on the new trail will appreciate your efforts, and skiers will also be thankful you have stayed off an established ski trail.

For trails with no visible signs of snowshoe tracks, try to stay to the far right on the way in and the same side on the way back out. The right side is an arbitrary choice; however, it is probable that skiers will use the right side on the way in, when they are moving at the slower speed, and the left on the way out, when they are moving much faster. Using one side for both directions of snowshoe travel may help to eliminate collisions. If snowshoers get into the habit of using the right side going in, a rule of etiquette may develop over time. This will invariably make life easier for all winter travellers and minimize conflict. Note that snowshoers should always use the same track going in and out, whereas

33

There is plenty of room for separate tracks on the way to the Burstall Lakes.

skiers may choose to make a separate trail for their return trip to avoid skiing into one another.

Regarding trail-breaking on any trail, a point of contention may arise after a heavy snowfall has sufficiently covered an established trail. In this situation the responsibility of trail-breaking falls upon the first party to start along the trail. If at all possible, snowshoers should try to avoid breaking trail over what might have been a ski track before the new snow arrived. Again, staying well over to the right side may be the best solution.

Simple common courtesy and decency, however, should be enough to avert any conflict between the different types of winter travellers. Remember we all share a common goal – to enjoy the beauty of the mountains.

Official Ski Trails

Groomed trails specifically for cross-country skiers are a little different from unofficial ski trails, such as the one to Burstall Pass. Snowshoers should try to avoid groomed trails completely. Damage to these trails, especially early in the season, can be dangerous to skiers who might ski into a hole made by snowshoers or hikers. Serious injury can result from such a ski accidents. Later in the season, these trails are usually well packed down and less susceptible to serious damage, but snowshoers should still stay away from them.

There are exceptions to this general rule. Some groomed trails provide the only access into certain areas. If this is the case, it may be necessary for snowshoers to use the trails, but they should always minimize the amount of time spent on them. Fortunately, for the most part, these trails are very wide, and getting in the way of skiers shouldn't be an issue. The trails leading out from the Mount Shark parking lot are good examples.

Avoid the following areas if possible:

1. Elk Pass (except the official snowshoe trail)

2. Pocaterra
3. Shark (except to see the south end of Spray Lake and Watridge Lake)

There are plenty of places to snowshoe in the Rockies without resorting to groomed trails. Be considerate and stay away from them.

Official Snowshoe Trails

Since the first edition of this book, Alberta Parks and Parks Canada have done an excellent job in creating more official snowshoe trails in the Canadian Rockies. This is especially true in Kananaskis. Official trails are a great place to start for beginners. They are usually relatively flat and short and have few to no objective hazards. Several of the official maps associated with these trails are included in this edition.

Right of Way

This point of etiquette is a simple one to practise and far less potentially contentious than the trail-breaking issue. Very simply, parties that travel faster have the right of way. For example, skiers are faster than snowshoers. Even on level or uphill terrain, skiers move at a slightly faster speed. Always be aware of this and move over to the right side of the trail to let skiers pass if required. Hopefully, you'll be on different trails so moving over won't be necessary.

Obviously, the difference in speed between skiers and snowshoers is far more pronounced when going downhill. Try to stay to the correct side of the trail and make yourself visible to skiers when going down through treed terrain. Wearing brightly coloured clothing is always a good idea. When in treed terrain, moving completely off the trail to let skiers pass is the best course of action.

Snowmobilers and Snowmobile Trails

The etiquette of right of way applies doubly when you encounter snowmobilers. Not only should you move over for them but you should also get completely off the trail when they approach and pass. If this happens to put you in a metre and a half of snow, so be it! Snowmobilers can move at terrific speeds. Being struck by a fast-moving, 80-kilogram skier would be very unpleasant; being struck by that same 80-kilogram person atop a 260-kilogram snowmobile, both moving at 60 km/h, would ruin your day in a big way! Snowmobiles are very noisy and so you will be afforded plenty of warning that one is coming your way. Try to make yourself visible to snowmobilers, even when you are well off the trail.

Snowmobiling is not permitted in Banff and Jasper National Parks, nor is it allowed in most areas of the Kananaskis region. For routes in this book, you are only likely to encounter snowmobilers in the Bragg Creek area.

Note that snowshoeing on snowmobile tracks is an accepted practice, unlike snowshoeing on ski tracks.

Technology

The days of navigating mountain terrain with a map, compass and a healthy dose of fear that you may get lost and never see humanity again are fading rapidly, if not completely gone. From an idealistic standpoint, everyone would know how to get around using these "old-school" (but also "good-school") methods. In reality, however, advances in technology have rendered them not obsolete or undesirable but simply impractical. In addition to a map and a compass, my gear now routinely includes three additional forms of navigational technologies: a handheld GPS, a SPOT device and my cellphone.

GPS

Global Positioning System has revolutionized the way we move around this planet. GPS uses satellites orbiting the earth to triangulate your exact position, down to the nearest metre. It is remarkably accurate and reliable these days. Some form of

Some serious avalanche terrain behind me on Smutwood Peak. We didn't go any farther that day.

built-in GPS is now the standard on many cars, cellphones and even cameras.

Most mountain enthusiasts now carry a handheld GPS unit. While older units were limited to giving location coordinates (GR numbers or latitude and longitude coordinates), with some route-mapping features, the newer models will pretty much do everything, except make your breakfast! Most GPS units now show your exact location and elevation on a topographical map, allow you to download routes and waypoints into the unit, and allow you to access geocaching information.

SPOT

SPOT stands for Satellite Personal Tracker and has widely become the weapon of choice for location tracking and for calling for help if necessary. The device uses a GPS signal to communicate with satellites and so a phone signal is not required. You can also use SPOT to notify friends and family of your GPS position and status, mark waypoints or track your progress on Google Maps. The device is extremely light and easy to use and the yearly fee is a very small price to pay for the peace of mind and access to help that SPOT gives you.

Up to late 2016, I have yet to use my SPOT for an emergency, but I will never go into the mountains without it anymore. SPOT can save your life – period!

Cellphones

I obstinately denied myself a cellphone ("mobile phone" for all my dashing relatives in England) until 2010, but now that I have the little gizmo, it's hard to imagine life without one. I likewise denied myself the use of that phone in the mountains until late 2013, but now that I do use it … you get the picture!

Very simply, the cellphone has single-handedly replaced the need for maps, a compass and for some even a separate GPS unit. Utilizing satellite signals, not cellphone signals, the Topographic Maps Canada app on my phone shows a topographical map and pinpoints my exact location on that map, all far out of the range that any cellphone signal can reach. Newer versions of this app include trail and mountain routes and greater map detail.

As well, cellphone signals are now reaching areas that were previously unreachable. I've been shocked and pleasantly surprised on many occasions to find myself FaceTiming my nephews and niece atop some fairly remote mountains.

The major limitation of cellphones in the mountains, and especially in regards to this book, is cold weather. The lithium-ion battery that most cellphones use for power drains much faster in cold weather. In fact, even with a full charge, your cellphone can lose power within minutes in very cold temperatures – a compelling argument for never relying solely on a phone in the mountains. Carry your phone as close to your body as possible to keep it warm.

At present, other inadequacies of cellphones in the mountains include the inability to call for help and lack of versatility when compared to GPS. However, it is certainly within the realm of possibility that in the near future a single cellphone will have the capabilities of all the above devices and it will become the only unit that a person carries.

Apps

In addition to the Topographic Maps Canada app, here are a few other apps you may find useful:

1. ViewRanger – similar to the Maps Canada app but also allows you to upload and download routes onto your phone.
2. SunCalc – great app that displays sunrise, sunset and the path of the sun on a topo map, for any day of the year. Very useful in helping to decide what time of day and what time of year to do routes, in order to get the best sun.
3. Accuweather – weather forecasts for all mountain areas pertinent to this book.

4. Avalanche.ca – not especially important for this book, but always worth having.

But Don't Forget the Classics

As wonderful as the technological world can be, "overwhelming" is also often an appropriate adjective to describe it. Embracing technology is a good thing, but relying on it completely may not be. Self-reliance in the mountains is paramount, and that includes the ability to navigate the terrain without the latest gizmo or app.

Personally, I love all the new technologies, but with all the new tools available to me, a paper map and compass have been, presently are and probably always will be in my backpack on every trip I take into the mountains. As stated, "old school but good school"!

Beyond Beginner Snowshoeing

Where do you go from here? If you have exhausted all the beginner routes around the Rockies and are looking to "step it up" into the world of intermediate and advanced snowshoeing, there are several steps to take.

First and foremost is to take an Avalanche Safety Training (AST) 1 course. This course will teach you the basics of avalanche assessment, avoiding avalanches and using beacons, probes and shovels. After honing your skills with AST 1, AST 2 is strongly recommended. You may eventually decide that you are happy to keep things simple by steering clear of all avalanche terrain. At least, having taken an AST 1 course, you will have the knowledge you need to make informed decisions about terrain. Thus, you will have the option to leave the beaten path and explore a little without putting yourself and others in harm's way.

Once you have an avalanche course under your belt, it's time to enroll in a mountaineering course. The Snow and Ice Long Weekend, offered by several companies, is highly recommended. In this course you will learn the fundamentals of glacier travel and rescue, using crampons and an ice axe, self-arrest and other valuable skills. Note that this and AST courses are general in scope and not geared specifically toward snowshoers. Check out the websites for Yamnuska Mountain Adventures (http://yamnuska.com), University of Calgary Outdoor Centre (https://www.ucalgary.ca/ActiveLiving/registration/Browse/All/Avalanche?filters=Outdoor-Centre) and Try That (www.trythat.ca/experiences/Alberta/Land/mountaineering) for more details on the Snow and Ice Long Weekend.

The third type of course you'll want to look into is an introduction to rock climbing. Rope-work, belayed climbing, using anchors, rappelling and the basics of rock-climbing technique are the primary focus of this course. An average snowshoe trip will not likely require you to employ any of the skills learned in a rock-climbing course (certainly they will not be necessary for trips in this guidebook), but the acquired skills and knowledge will be invaluable to those looking to widen their experience in the mountains and reach new levels of achievement.

With AST, mountaineering and climbing courses under your belt you are granted almost unlimited potential in your mountain adventures.

Conclusion

Hopefully, the preceding text has not only been informative but also served to pique your interest in the exciting activity of snowshoeing. Snowshoeing can be as simple or as complex as you want it to be. However, regardless of the level of trip you are undertaking, it is extremely important to be informed about the dangers of the environment, etiquette in that environment and choosing appropriate objectives for the conditions and your skill level. The Canadian Rockies is an inherently dangerous environment, but snowshoeing in the Rockies does not have to be a dangerous activity. Be informed, be sensible and have fun! Enjoy the trips to follow.

The Trips

The routes in this book cover many areas of the southern Canadian Rockies, from majestic Waterton in the far south to the amazing environs around Bow Lake, about 500 kilometres farther northwest. The lack of routes in some areas does not mean they are not snowshoe friendly – it simply means I have yet to explore those areas fully. The Kananaskis area is heavily favoured, simply because snowshoe routes in Kananaskis are easy to get to, and there are plenty of them. The snow, especially in the southwest section of Kananaskis, comes early and stays late. Kananaskis also has the greatest concentration of official snowshoe trails.

Each area detailed below offers opportunities for the easy snowshoe trips outlined in this guidebook and the serious snowshoe-mountaineering trips described in *Snowshoeing in the Canadian Rockies, 2nd Edition*. Needless to say, the scenery and views throughout the Rockies are fantastic, regardless of the area you choose. Personally, my favourite destinations for beginner snowshoeing routes are Highway 742 in Kananaskis and Yoho. However, each area has several awesome trips that are worthy of multiple visits.

Two final reminders before you set out: read the introductory information for each trip carefully so you are aware of the level and demands of the trip; and check the weather forecast before you set out.

You are now ready to explore one of the most magical environments this planet has to offer – enjoy!

Bragg Creek and Elbow Valley

Bragg Creek's close proximity to Calgary and the nature of the terrain around and to the west of the hamlet make it an ideal area to explore in the winter. Unfortunately, its easterly location also welcomes snow-eating chinook winds. Picking an appropriate time of year to put on the snowshoes can be the biggest challenge for trips around Bragg Creek. January through March are generally the most reliable months for good snow, although a warm stretch of weather can melt most of the snow at any time of the year. Conversely, a heavy snowfall may allow trips in December or April. A good strategy is to pick a trip in this area immediately after a major snowfall. Needless to say, this may render the drive difficult and/or dangerous. Be sure to check the AMA road reports before setting out.

If you are doing any trips in the vicinity of the seasonal road closure just beyond the Elbow Falls parking lot (December 1 to May 15 each year), consider an enjoyable winter walk around the falls as a finish to your day. Although they won't be giving Niagara Falls a run for their money, Elbow Falls look fantastic in the dead of winter when there have been enough cold hours for the spray from the falling water to create fascinating ice sculptures alongside the river. You can complete the entire falls walk in 5 minutes if time is a concern. However, better to take your time and enjoy the scenery. Note that this is not a snowshoe trip and can easily be completed in hiking boots.

Enjoying the view from Mustang Hills.

1 Snowshoe Hare Loop

This is an official snowshoe trail that provides a pleasant up-and-down stroll through forest. Don't expect any far-reaching views, and given the easterly location of the route, snowshoes may not be necessary at any time of the year. Note that because the trail is in an environmentally sensitive area, it is closed from April 1–November 30.

DIFFICULTY: intermediate

ELEVATION LOSS/GAIN: minimal

ROUND-TRIP DISTANCE: 5.4 km

ROUND-TRIP TIME: 1.5–2.5 hours

MAPS: 82 J/15 Bragg Creek, Gem Trek Bragg Creek and Elbow Valley (Sheep Valley)

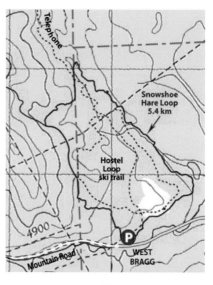

Directions

Drive west on Highway 22 to Bragg Creek and turn right, onto Balsam Avenue, following the sign to West Bragg Creek. In 500 m turn left on Centre Avenue and drive 8.7 km to the trailhead. Park at the east end of the large parking lot.

The loop can be done in either direction: counter-clockwise, starting from the east end of the parking lot, or clockwise, starting nearer the west end. Toss a coin to pick one.

Route descriptions for both directions are unnecessary, as it is simply a matter of following the orange snowshoe signs. If you go in a clockwise direction, be careful not to jump onto one of the ski trails when you arrive at a couple of junctions early on. Other than that, route-finding is not an issue and travel is generally very easy. A few steeper sections that give the trip its intermediate rating may require some extra care, but they are very short.

ABOVE: *Map of the Snowshoe Hare Loop by Gillean Daffern. TOP RIGHT: Nina Van snowshoes through pleasant forested terrain.*

OPPOSITE: *Mack and Michael at one of the many snowshoe signs along the way. Behind the boys, Abbey the dog is vole hunting – yum, yum! (Ken Schmaltz)*

2 Snowy Owl

Kudos go to the Greater Bragg Creek Trails Association for designing this delightful snowshoe trail. The scenery and terrain are varied and interesting throughout. As well, there are options to do a quick 1.5-hour trip or a longer more involved one, up to 4.5 hours. The best time to do the trip is right after a major snowfall, and Alberta Parks recommends that you not snowshoe or hike the trail before November 30 and after April 1. Bring Microspikes if you have them, just in case the trail is more Icy Owl than Snowy Owl (groan!).

A trip at dusk yields some interesting clouds and lighting.

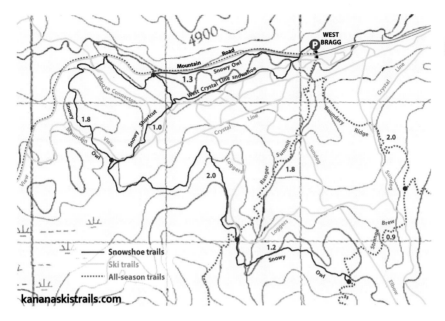

*Map of all the Snowy Owl Routes
(map courtesy of kananaskistrails.com).*

DIFFICULTY: intermediate

ELEVATION GAIN: 80–200 m

ROUND-TRIP DISTANCE: 5.4–12.2 km

ROUND-TRIP TIME: 1.5–3.5 hours

MAPS: 82 J/15 Bragg Creek, Gem Trek
Bragg Creek and Elbow Valley (Sheep
Valley)

Directions

Drive west on Highway 22 to Bragg Creek
and turn right, onto Balsam Avenue, following the sign to West Bragg Creek. In 500 m
turn left on Centre Avenue and drive 8.7 km
to the trailhead. Park at the west end of the
large parking lot. Hike out onto the main
road (blockaded during the winter) and turn
right (west), reaching the first snowshoe
sign in about 100 m, on the left side of the
road. From here on in, a detailed route description is unnecessary, due to the terrific
placement of snowshoe signs. Some 1.4 km
down the trail you will have to decide on

your specific route. There are three potential
routes to take from here (see map):

Route 1: A small loop via the first section of
Snowy Owl and then Snowy Shortcut
back to the main trail – 5.4 km and approximately 1.5–2 hours.

Route 2: Snowy Owl to its end and then
back the same way, but using Snowy
Shortcut – 12.2 km and approximately
3.5–4.5 hours.

Route 3: A big loop via Snowy Owl to its end
and then Strange Brew and Boundary
Ridge, all the way back to the parking
lot – 9.2 km and approximately 2.5–3.5
hours.

The big loop (Route 3) is highly recommended. This route allows you to see the
most and get a good workout.

Here are a few points to keep in mind
for all routes:

• Trail signs and snowshoe signs are
plentiful and easy to follow.

45

- The first section of the Snowy Owl is arguably the most interesting part of the day, so don't skip it.
- Fat-tire bikers often use the trail. Be on the lookout for them and give them the right of way as they pass.
- The trail throughout can get very icy at any time during the snow season. If there is not enough snow to snowshoe, at least bring another type of traction device such as Microspikes.
- If you choose Route 3, follow Strange Brew and Boundary Ridge (north) and avoid using the ski trails.

3 Ranger Ridge

Ranger Ridge is a short extension of the very popular Fullerton Loop route. As such the Fullerton section is often well packed down, and snowshoes may not be necessary. That being said the well-travelled terrain often becomes icy. Snowshoes or spikes can be useful if that is the case.

DIFFICULTY: intermediate

ELEVATION GAIN: approximately 300 m

ROUND-TRIP DISTANCE: 8 km

ROUND-TRIP TIME: 2.5–4.5 hours

MAPS: 82 J/15 Bragg Creek, Gem Trek Bragg Creek and Elbow Valley (Sheep Valley)

Directions

From the four-way stop in Bragg Creek, drive south on Highway 22 for a few kilometres and turn right (west) onto Highway 66. Drive 9.7 km to the Allen Bill parking lot. Park at the east end of this popular starting point.

The trail starts at the east end, going east and then turning north, under the highway, alongside the Elbow River. After paralleling the river for a short distance, the trail veers a little to the left and passes through a cattle gate. More easy snowshoeing/hiking leads to the well-signed Fullerton Loop, 1.1 km from the parking lot. Turn left onto the wide trail.

After crossing the first bridge and just before the second bridge, the trail forks (300 m from the Fullerton Loop turnoff and unsigned as of 2012). Either fork goes, as they

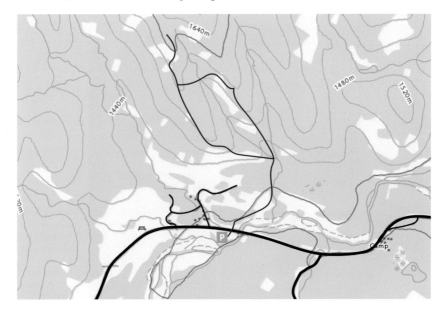

are both part of the same loop, but a clockwise direction is preferable. Turn left onto the fork and snowshoe or hike the easy-to-follow trail, taking in improving views to the southwest as you gain elevation.

When you arrive at the second wooden bench, you've also attained the high point / viewpoint of the loop. From here you can continue to follow the loop as it turns east, or for a little more exercise and some additional views, complete the short extension of the trip up the west side of Ranger Ridge.

Extension up the West Side of Ranger Ridge

Leave the main trail at the loop high point and travel northwest up and through a brief section of light forest to an open area. Continue up to the treed ridge above and travel along the edge of the trees. This eventually leads to another open area that you will probably want to call your high point for the day. The views aren't much different from those at the loop high point, so you'll be doing this extension mostly for the exercise. An option does exist to continue on to the high point to the northwest, but it is fully treed and has very limited views. Most parties will choose to turn around and complete the remainder of the Fullerton Loop back to the Allen Bill parking lot.

Not enough snow on the trail for snowshoeing, but the atmospheric clouds made up for that.

4 Prairie Mountain

A snowshoe ascent of Prairie Mountain is a terrific way to transition from beginner snowshoeing to intermediate snowshoeing. The ascent has no avalanche risk and is not committing in any way. However, it has a decent amount of horizontal distance to cover, a relatively large elevation gain and enough steep terrain to acquaint the beginner snowshoer with some of the elements of higher-level snowshoeing. Yet again the crux of the trip is waiting for enough snow to accumulate so that snowshoes are actually necessary. Best to make an attempt right after a big dump of snow. Take Microspikes as an alternative to snowshoes.

DIFFICULTY: advanced

MOUNTAIN HEIGHT: 2210 m

ELEVATION GAIN: 700 m

ROUND-TRIP DISTANCE: 7 km

ROUND-TRIP TIME: 4–6 hours

MAPS: 82 J/15 Bragg Creek, Gem Trek Bragg Creek and Elbow Valley (Sheep Valley)

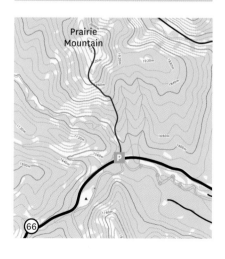

Directions

From the four-way stop in Bragg Creek, drive south on Highway 22 for a few kilometres and turn right (west) onto Highway 66. Drive about 18.4 km west to the road closure and park on the side of the road, but not in front of the gate. Walk or snowshoe west for about 100 m to a point just before Prairie Creek flows under the road. Gaining Prairie Mountain's south ridge here may actually be the crux of the trip. Turn sharply right (northeast) and make your way up steep, potentially rocky terrain to gain the plateau above. There is also a less steep but longer route that side-slopes the ridge, eventually arriving at the same plateau (see photo).

The trail now heads north, through treed terrain for a fair distance. Throughout, the route is obvious and probably well-travelled. Open areas occasionally reveal sections of the upper part of the mountain to the northwest.

Eventually the trail turns more northwest and starts up much steeper terrain, again through the trees. This is where your snowshoes will be very helpful for traction if the trail is icy or snowy. Grind your way up the steep slopes, popping out in open

ABOVE: *Dinah Kruze takes the alternative route to gain the plateau. (Bob Spirko)*

OPPOSITE ABOVE: *Dinah reaches an open area along the way. The route ascends the treed slope in front from right to left and then goes north to the summit. (Bob Spirko)*

OPPOSITE BELOW: *The classic curve of Prairie's upper ridge. (Bob Spirko)*

terrain about 1 km south of the summit. Turn right (north) and make your way to the huge cairn at the top. This part of the trip is prone to be wind-blasted and snowshoes will probably not be necessary.

The summit view features Moose Mountain to the north, Powderface Ridge and Nihahi Ridge to the southwest, and the Banded Peak quartet farther southwest. Return the way you came. Descending the steep sections will be much easier with snowshoes.

Highway 40 South

Highway 40 South does not boast the same number of snowshoe routes as its counterpart to the west – Highway 742 (Smith–Dorrien) (see page 60). Nevertheless, there are several worthwhile trips in the area and, the easterly location of this road makes it a good place to find good weather when the situation is more dismal farther west. This is especially true of the north section of the road, which may be basking in sunlight while clouds consume more westerly peaks. The north section is also subject to snow-eating blasts from chinook winds. You may end up carrying your snowshoes as much as you wear them.

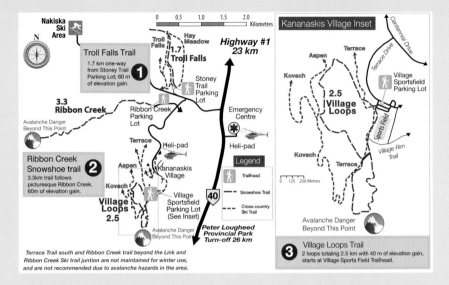

Map labels:

Nakiska Ski Area

N

0 0.5 1.0 1.5 2.0
Kilometres

Troll Falls Trail
1.7 km one-way from Stoney Trail Parking Lot; 60 m of elevation gain. **1**

Troll Falls

Hay Meadow

1.7 Troll Falls

Highway #1 23 km

Stoney Trail Parking Lot

3.3 Ribbon Creek

Ribbon Creek Parking Lot

Terrace

Emergency Centre

Heli-pad

Heli-pad

Avalanche Danger Beyond This Point

Ribbon Creek Snowshoe trail **2**
3.3km trail follows picturesque Ribbon Creek. 60m of elevation gain.

Terrace

Aspen

Kananaskis Village

Kovach

Village Loops 2.5

Village Sportsfield Parking Lot (See Inset)

40

Avalanche Danger Beyond This Point

Peter Lougheed Provincial Park Turn-off 26 km

Legend

Trailhead

— — — Snowshoe Trail

- - - - Cross-country Ski Trail

Terrace Trail south and Ribbon Creek trail beyond the Link and Ribbon Creek Ski trail juntion are not maintained for winter use, and are not recommended due to avalanche hazards in the area.

Kananaskis Village Inset

Centennial Drive

Terrace Drive

Aspen

Terrace

Kovach

2.5 Village Loops

Village Sportsfield Parking Lot

Sports Field

Kovach

Village Rim Trail

Terrace

0 125 250 Metres

Avalanche Danger Beyond This Point

Village Loops Trail **3**
2 loops totaling 2.5 km with 40 m of elevation gain, starts at Village Sports Field Trailhead.

ABOVE: *The easy snowshoe routes around Kananaskis Village (map courtesy of Alberta Parks, Kananaskis).*

BELOW: *Nina Van snowoes the scenic Kananaskis Village Trail. Tlhe awesome form of Mount Kidd is cto the left. The hill above Nina's head is the former Mount Kidd Fire Lookout – another advanced trip described in* Snowshoeing in the Canadian Rockies.

5 Troll Falls

This short trip goes to a small frozen waterfall. It is an ideal trip for the family and young children. Yet again, waiting for sufficient snow coverage will be the key to making this a snowshoe trip instead of an icy hike.

DIFFICULTY: easy

ELEVATION GAIN: 60 m

ROUND-TRIP DISTANCE: 3.7 km

ROUND-TRIP TIME: 1.5–2 hours

MAPS: 82 J/14 Spray Lakes Reservoir, Gem Trek Canmore and Kanaskis Village

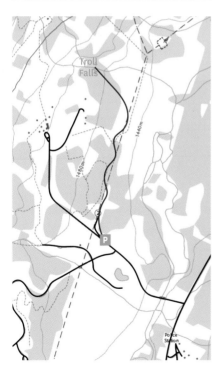

Directions

Drive south on Highway 40 for about 25 km to the Kananaskis Village turnoff. Turn right and drive about 1 km up the road. Turn right on the gravel road, signed "Stoney Trailhead." The parking area is a few hundred metres down the road.

Snowshoe north on Stoney Trail for about 1.2 km. At the intersection with Hay Meadow Trail, turn left and snowshoe a few hundred metres to Troll Falls Trail. A short section of the trail is groomed for cross-country skiers, so stay to the side. Follow the trail and signs to Troll Falls in about 600 m. At the falls, you can actually crawl right behind the frozen water! Return the same way you came in.

ABOVE: *The frozen form of Troll Falls.*

BELOW: *Mark crawls behind the falls.*

6 Kananaskis Village Snowshoe Trail

This short loop route through the forests above Kananaskis Village has several pleasant viewpoints. Even though snow may be scarce at various times of the year and/or after a chinook, the trail tends to get icy. Therefore, snowshoes or spikes are recommended for the entire trip. Consider combining this short jaunt with another trip in the area, or just relax in Woody's Pub for refreshments afterward (no minors!).

DIFFICULTY: intermediate

ELEVATION GAIN: approximately 100 m

ROUND-TRIP DISTANCE: 2.7 km, figure-eight loop

ROUND-TRIP TIME: 45–90 minutes

MAPS: 82 J/14 Spray Lakes Reservoir, Gem Trek Canmore and Kananaskis Village

Directions

Driving south on Highway 40, turn right at the Nakiska turnoff. Shortly after, turn left toward Kananaskis Village. Just before the village, turn right at the sign for Mount Kidd Manor and follow the road to the public parking lot. From the parking lot you'll be able to take in a good view of Mount Kidd.

Family snowshoeing around Kananaskis Village. Most of the time Rogan enjoys riding in the chariot, but sometimes he just wants to do the work himself.

The loop can be completed in either direction. The north loop has the most elevation gain, but the south has better views. To start with the north loop, find the trailhead at the west end of the parking lot and look for the first orange snowshoe sign on a light-blue pole. (The south loop starts with a similar marker, but it is slightly to the south (left) of the west end of the parking lot.) Go to the start of the north loop and follow the snowshoe signs through the trees in a northwesterly direction. The remainder of the route is simply a matter of following a string of snowshoe signs and orange and pink flagging in the trees.

The high point of the north loop has a good view of the northeast side of Mount Kidd and of the ascent slopes to Mount Kidd Lookout (a trip to which is described in *Snowshoeing in the Canadian Rockies*). The trail soon swings around to the south and descends to a junction where the south loop starts.

Again, follow signs and flagging around the shorter south loop, enjoying some very respectable views of mountains to the south and east. At the south end of the loop, do not be tempted to follow the ski tracks going south. This path may put you in avalanche danger.

Looking southeast across Kananaskis Valley toward The Wedge. (Gillean Daffern)

Highway 742 (Smith–Dorrien)

This stretch of highway from Canmore to the Kananaskis Lakes Trail turnoff is an absolute gold mine of snowshoeing potential. I think it is the best location in the southern end of the Canadian Rockies for snowshoeing. You can park your vehicle almost anywhere along this road and find an interesting route or area to snowshoe in; just don't park in any of the "no stopping" zones because they are avalanche areas. Returning to find your vehicle buried in several metres of avalanche debris may put a damper on your day!

When other areas of the Rockies, especially those to the east, are struggling to maintain a good base of snow, the routes along the Smith–Dorrien are usually swimming in the white stuff. Great snowshoeing snow is almost guaranteed, especially from January to May. If you are looking for deep snow and lots of it, this is the place to go.

Highway 742 can be accessed from the southwest end of Canmore or via Highway 40 South and Kananaskis Trail. If you are coming from Calgary, the driving time to Chester Lake and Burstall Pass parking lots is about the same using either route. Therefore any routes north of those parking lots can be more quickly accessed by going through Canmore, and routes to the south from Highway 40 South and Kananaskis Trail.

Also, note that Highway 742 is a gravel road and can be quite snowy and slippery after a snowfall. And then when all that snow melts, the road gets muddy and slippery – an equally bad combination.

Even the snowmen need snowshoes in this area! Michelle Marche, Nicole Lisafeld and their new buddy make their way across Burstall Lakes. (Sadly, about a month later, the snowman drowned in his own bodily fluids.)

7 Rummel Lake

Rummel Lake is an excellent destination for snowshoers and ski-ers alike. Its popularity means that a trail will most likely be broken for you, but if not, be prepared for some serious work. Take along a companion (or four) to ease the strain! There is a winter backcountry campground at Rummel Lake for those who wish to make this a multi-day trip. A permit to camp is required and can be picked up at any national or provincial park information centre.

DIFFICULTY: intermediate
ELEVATION GAIN: 350 m
ROUND-TRIP DISTANCE: 10 km
ROUND-TRIP TIME: 5–7 hours
MAPS: 82 J/14 Spray Lakes Reservoir, Gem Trek Canmore, Gem Trek Kanan-askis Lakes

Directions

Park on the east side of Highway 742, oppos-ite the turnoff to Engadine Lodge, about 6.3 km north of the Chester Lake parking lot.

The trail quickly ascends into the trees and then parallels the highway, heading SSE. After several hundred metres it turns back on itself, now heading northeast.

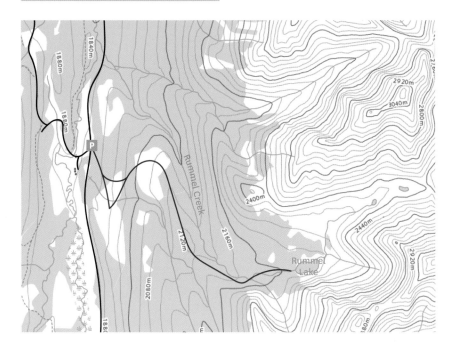

ABOVE: *The view to the southwest. The big peak at the far right is Mount Birdwood. (Marko Stavric)*

BELOW: *Rummel Lake. (Matthew Clay)*

There is a small shortcut before the turn that you may be able to take if the trail is broken. Soon the terrain opens up a little, revealing pleasant views to the west.

The trail then swings around and heads southeast. Eventually it goes back into the trees, following a ridge high above Rummel Creek. Stay on this ridge as it starts to curve around to the east toward Rummel Lake, losing a little elevation along the way. Cross to the north side of Rummel Creek, around GR192324, and follow the creek or perhaps

The view to the northwest from near the top of the second cutblock. (Gillean Daffern)

a well-packed snowshoe trail east of the west side of Rummel Lake. Return the same way you came in. Note that extending your day by going into the beautiful valley to the northeast exposes you to avalanche terrain and is therefore not recommended for beginners without avalanche training and equipment.

8 Marushka Lake

This trip has respectable views of the Spray Lake area en route to Marushka Lake, although they are inferior to those experienced from the middle of Spray Lake. The route steers clear of the avalanche terrain on Tent Ridge, is generally easy to follow and provides a few hours of good exercise. The scenery at Marushka Lake is somewhat anticlimactic, as snow cover will hide the wonderful colours of the water. To see those colours and complete the extension to Kirsten Tarns, see Gillean Daffern's Kananaskis Country Trail Guide, Volume 1, *and do the trip in the summer. Also note that the net elevation loss for this trip does not necessarily mean you will race to the lake in record time. If you are breaking trail, the trip can be more strenuous than expected.*

DIFFICULTY: intermediate

ELEVATION LOSS/GAIN: 36–68 m

ROUND-TRIP DISTANCE: 8 km

ROUND-TRIP TIME: 3.5–5 hours

MAPS: 82 J/14 Spray Lakes Reservoir, Gem Trek Kanaskis Lakes

Directions

Drive south on Highway 742, and turn right at the Engadine Lodge turnoff; then drive 1.8 km to a small parking area on the right side of the road.

Hike about 100 m farther up the road, put on your snowshoes and turn left onto the obvious logging road. This route is also the start of the path to Tent Ridge and is very popular with backcountry skiers. Stay

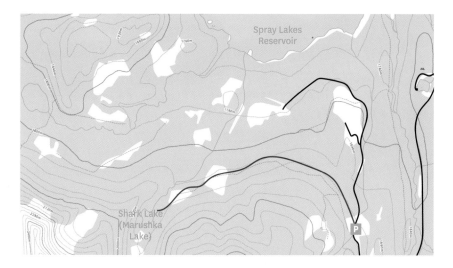

ABOVE: *On a not so clear day there still may be some interesting views to take in. Looking east from the trail: Mount Buller at the left and Mount Bogart, enjoying some sun, to the right.*

BELOW: *On a clear day, the view to Mount Shark is excellent. (Bernie Nemeth)*

off their ski tracks, even if this means a strenuous trail-break of your own. There's tons of room for both sets of tracks.

Snowshoe the logging road for about 20 minutes to where the road forks. Stay on the main road (right fork). The left fork leads to Tent Ridge. Stay right again, about 20–25 minutes later, when another path drifts off to the left. There is flagging on the trees here to guide you. The trail eventually curves around the hillside and becomes less obvious where the trees are starting to reassert themselves. Stay at more or less the same elevation, taking a path of least resistance in a southwesterly direction, toward the large and wonderful form of Mount Shark.

Finding the lake can be a little tricky if the trail hasn't been previously broken. Keep going southwest, sometimes gaining a little elevation and finally losing elevation to the east shore of the lake. As stated, the view at Marushka may fail to impress, but the lake is worth a visit at least once. Return the same way you came in.

9 South End of Spray Lake

The scenery around the southwest end of Spray Lake is anywhere from excellent to astonishing on a clear day. If you are lucky, the frozen surface of the lake may be wind-blasted clean in some areas, revealing outstanding ice scenery. Even if it isn't, the surrounding mountains will be fantastic.

DIFFICULTY: easy

ELEVATION LOSS/GAIN: approximately 100 m

ROUND-TRIP DISTANCE: approximately 4–8 km

ROUND-TRIP TIME: 2 hours

MAPS: 82 J/14 Spray Lakes Reservoir, Gem Trek Canmore

Directions

Driving south on Highway 742, turn right at the Engadine Lodge turnoff and follow the road to the Mount Shark parking lot.

The first order of business is to make it down to Spray Lake. This can be accomplished by following a maze of ski trails. Be considerate to skiers on these groomed trails and stay off to the side. You need to locate the Watridge Lake trailhead, which is at the northwest end of the parking lot.

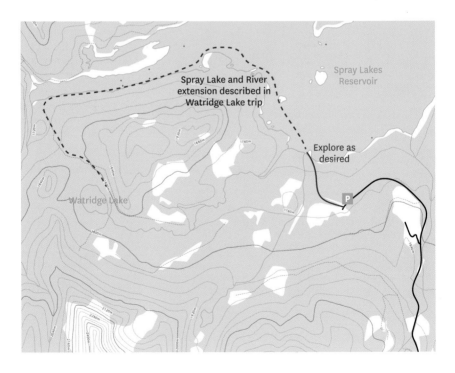

ABOVE: *Checking out the ice, with Cone Mountain in the background.*

RIGHT: *Cracks and bubbles in Spray Lake's ice.*

The trail descends immediately for a few metres and then heads west in a straight line. Follow this for about 500 m. Turn right at the first intersection, ascend a short hill and then turn left onto a trail that immediately descends toward Spray Lake. Follow this down, and when it curves around to the west (left), turn right, into the trees, and make your way to the lake in a matter of minutes.

At the shore of Spray Lake, Mount Fortune is immediately visible across the lake, appearing as a low, rounded hump. Aiming for Fortune is a good impulse, but you can generally go in any direction. Point yourself toward Fortune (NNW) and off you go. There are several small islands in the middle of the lake, so don't be alarmed when you start going slightly uphill.

The southwest end of Spray Lake can be an interesting and fulfilling adventure in itself, depending on the weather and the state of the ice. Windblown sections of the lake surface may be free of snow, revealing huge cracks in the ice, as well as air bubbles and other fascinating phenomena. In other parts, huge slabs of ice may have collided with each other as they expanded while freezing, pushing each other up in a process similar to that of mountain building. Of course, the lake may be covered in deep snow with no exposed ice at all, in which

Approaching one of the islands in the middle of the lake. From left to right the peaks are Tent Ridge, Mount Smuts and Mount Shark.

case you'll have even more time to enjoy magnificent panoramas of the surrounding mountains. Tent Ridge, Smuts, Shark, Morrison, Turner and Cone may be particularly eye-catching, especially on a clear day.

10 Watridge Lake

This is a terrific beginner trip on a "highway" of a trail that is super easy to follow. After a rewarding view of Watridge Lake, back-dropped by shapely Cone Mountain, a quick visit to Karst Springs is sweet icing on the cake! And for those who really want to experience the area, the Spray River extension is outstanding.

DIFFICULTY: easy to the lake, advanced to Karst Springs, intermediate for the Spray River Extension

LAKE HEIGHT: 1800 m

ELEVATION GAIN: 60 m

ROUND-TRIP DISTANCE: 7.4 km

ROUND-TRIP TIME: 2.5–4 hours

MAPS: 82 J/14 Spray Lakes Reservoir, Gem Trek Canmore, Gem Trek Kananaskis Lakes

Directions

Driving south on Highway 742, turn right (west) at the Mount Shark – Engadine Lodge turnoff and follow the road to the Mount Shark parking lot. Follow the signs to Watridge Lake on the very wide, often groomed trail. The trail is about 30 m from the parking area. As always, DO NOT step on any ski tracks. There is tons of room to make a separate snowshoe track.

Additional instructions are not required once you are on your way. Simply follow

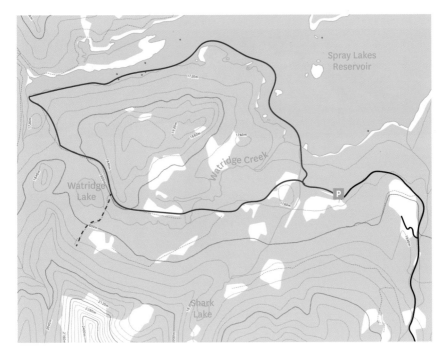

ABOVE: *Hopefully, snow covers the entire Karst Springs area except the vibrant green moss in the creek. (Nicole Lisafeld)*

BELOW: *A small taste of some of the wonderful scenery where the river meets the lake. Mount Fortune and Fortulent Peak are ascents described in the advanced snowshoeing book.*

ABOVE: *Three snowshoers make their way to Watridge Lake. The stunning forms of Old Goat Mountain and Mount Nestor provide a magnificent backdrop. (Peter Hopkins)*

BELOW: *Picturesque Mount Engadine keeps you company as you search for the spot to enter the trees where the ski trail lies. P=approximate point to go back into the trees.*

the signs to Watridge Lake, turning around once in a while to admire the peaks to the east and north. The peak straight ahead is Mount Shark. Alan Kane describes an excellent scramble route up this interesting peak.

A good pace will get you to the turnoff to the lake in about an hour (GR110344). There is the sign with a map on the right side of the trail. Take a sharp left turn and go downhill to reach the shores of Watridge Lake within minutes.

The view to the northwest of Cone Mountain's striking southeast end will likely be the highlight of the view from the lake. To the west sit the duo of Mount Turner (north) and Mount Morrison (south). They maybe look like one long mountain but have been given two names, in honour of Sir Richard Turner and Sir Edward Morrison, lieutenants who fought side by side in 1900 with the Royal Canadian Dragoons during the South African War. Mount Shark now lies to the southeast. Return the same way (once you have completed the mandatory extension to Karst Springs!) and/or do the Spray River/Lake extension, as described after the Karst Springs description.

Karst Springs

Some 400 horizontal and 75 vertical metres – for what you will see during the course of this short trip this is the "best bang for your buck" around! Karst Springs is not to be missed.

Directions

A large sign, by the lake, points you in the right direction. Cross the lake outlet on a narrow, wooden bridge and then continue following the trail into the forest. There is a boardwalk here to reduce damage to the fragile foliage, however it may be snow-covered. More than likely the trail will be broken, as this is a very popular destination year-round.

The trail meanders through the forest until it joins up with Karst Springs (to your left). Hopefully, the snow coverage will not be so great as to completely hide the amazingly vibrant green moss that covers almost everything in the spring (creek). Continue up the trail, taking in more terrific "mossy" scenes.

Quickly, the trail starts to gain elevation. Your snowshoe crampons will be a blessing here as you effortlessly ascend the often icy terrain that may thwart those who are simply on foot. Arrive at a wooden bench for another breathtaking view of the upper springs.

From the bench, the trail gets quite a bit steeper, as it switchbacks to the spring outlet. Those not used to such angles on snowshoes may want to call it a day at the bench. However, a good set of snowshoe crampons will make easy work of the ascent for those who are comfortable with the terrain. Use caution when reaching the end of the trail. There is a fence to prevent you from falling into the spring, but the snow can be piled high enough to render that fence completely ineffective. Enjoy the view looking down the spring and then return the same way.

Spray River and Spray Lake

This is a totally amazing extension of the Watridge Lake trip and highly, highly recommended. The route takes you down to Spray River and then onto Spray Lake, where you can follow the lake back to the parking lot. It's a fantastically scenic loop route. Don't underestimate it, however. Round-trip it's about 14 km (without Karst Springs) and will take approximately 4.5–6.5 hours, with 226 m of total elevation gain. A GPS will come in handy for finding the ski trail back to the parking lot, near the end of the trip, as will a few friends for trail-breaking duties.

Directions

After visiting Watridge Lake (and possibly Karst Springs) return up the hill to the main trail. Turn left and follow it for several kilometres, all the way down to a bridge over the Spray River. You will lose about 100 m of elevation along the way and may be wishing you had skis (at least for this part). Hopefully, you have been blessed with clear skies, because the view of the river and Cone Mountain, from the middle of the bridge, is breathtaking – far better than the similar view from Watridge Lake.

Return to the east side of the bridge and start following the river downstream (north). Be prepared for some strenuous trail-breaking if a trail has not already been carved out. Stay as close to the river as possible, without putting yourself in danger. Thankfully, an ice shelf along the river's edge soon appears. Travel will hopefully be much easier at this point, as the shelf gets blasted by the wind, reducing snow levels. The ice scenery by the river can be outstanding.

And so is the mountain scenery! The prominent mountain to the west is Mount Turner, but as the river turns east, a host of other magnificent mountains appear, seemingly in pairs: Fortune and Fortulent, Nestor and Old Goat, Buller and Engadine. There is never a dull moment at this end of the lake.

Depending on snow and ice conditions, you will soon realize that you are no longer following the river but are on the lake. A group of tree stumps (hopefully not snow-covered) at GR112369 marks this spot wonderfully. Continue going east, staying closer to the south side of the lake. As of early 2016, thin wooden stakes marked the route.

This part of the trip is deceivingly long. Snowshoe east until it is possible to turn south (GR128370), toward the southern-most point of the lake. Keep going south, aiming for GR135360. Upon reaching that point, head into the trees, looking for one of the ski trails. If your route-finding is good, it's only about 30 m through the trees onto a trail. Once you've found the ski trail, turn left and then follow your nose back to the Watridge Lake Trail and then back to the parking lot. These are dedicated ski trails and you should avoid being on them for too long.

11 Commonwealth Lake

The highlight of the trip will be the beautiful form of Commonwealth Peak behind its namesake lake. It is a short trip that can be completed in under 2 hours round-trip if the trail is well broken and packed down. For additional views and some pretty stunning scenery, you can go beyond the lake, but this will take you into avalanche terrain if you go too far up the valley.

DIFFICULTY: intermediate

LAKE ELEVATION: 2042 m

ELEVATION GAIN: 200 m

ROUND-TRIP DISTANCE: 4.6 km

ROUND-TRIP TIME: 2–4 hours

MAPS: 82 J/14 Spray Lakes Reservoir, Gem Trek Kananaskis Lakes

Directions

Note that this trip can also be accessed from Commonwealth Creek Logging Road.

Drive 2.2 km south of the Mount Shark – Engadine Lodge turnoff and park on the west side of the road, around GR176312. Look west, across the flats of Smuts Creek, for a small gap in the trees (see photo). Snowshoe across the flats and go through the gap. The path trends slightly right before arriving at a "No Camping/Fires" sign.

The gap in the trees is visible from the parking area. G=gap. S=Mount Smuts. TF=The Fist. TLR=Tryst Lake Ridge. ETR=East summit of Tent Ridge.

This is a very popular area so expect there to be a multitude of trails. As you approach the sign, go slightly left into the trees and head southwest. You'll soon arrive at another popular trail that runs north–south. The terrain opens up a little and the route should become more obvious.

At this point you should look for a cutline running southwest, south of Commonwealth Creek. To find it, follow the trail going toward the distinctive form of The Fist. The trail soon swings around to the left and then arrives at an open area, where it forks (GR168304). This fork is not always obvious. There are two routes to the lake from this important junction: via the summer trail or via a creek that drains the north end of the lake. For ascent, the summer is recommended.

Summer Trail

At the junction, take the left fork. If the trail is broken it will be easy to follow as it steeply winds its way uphill, traverses to the right for a short distance and then switchbacks up to a higher elevation. Eventually the trail turns right again and traverses the northwest slopes of Commonwealth Ridge, heading south. If you are breaking new trail, do your best to pick the safest line. This may entail gaining more elevation onto less steep slopes. Continue south for several hundred metres and then start to look to your right to spot the lake through the trees. Invariably you will have to lose a little elevation to reach the lake. You will probably descend to the east side of the lake around GR166297.

Creek Route

At the junction, take the right fork. This is the trail that more or less follows the left bank of Commonwealth Creek all the way up and into the Commonwealth valley. Follow this trail for a few hundred metres, at one point crossing a subsidiary creek coming down from the left. Shortly after crossing this creek, look for another less obvious creek at GR164301. This is the creek you will want to follow all the way up to the north end of Commonwealth Lake. At first it is best to follow the right bank of the creek, but higher up you will be forced right into the creek. Work your way up steeper slopes to the lake.

Commonwealth Peak (left) backdrops Commonwealth Lake. Pig's Back to the right.

For Both Routes

Hopefully, clear skies will grant you a terrific view of Commonwealth Peak and Pig's Back to the right of the peak. The best views are from the east and north sides of the lake so be sure to visit each side. At an elevation above 2000 m the lake will probably be frozen well into spring and can usually be crossed right down the middle.

For return, either go back the way you came or use the route you didn't ascend. The advantage of the Creek Route is that it is downhill all the way. To use that route,

go to the north end of the lake and snowshoe right down the middle of the creek. There are steep sections and you'll have to duck under a fallen tree or two, but travel is generally fast and easy. When the creek bed becomes less confined, move over to the left side of the creek and snowshoe along the bank. You'll eventually run into the trail that parallels Commonwealth Creek. Turn right and follow that trail back to the important junction.

If you came up via the Creek Route, using the Summer Trail really doesn't offer any

The exquisite scenery near the boulder field.

advantages – scenic or otherwise. I would use the Creek Route for descent also.

Extension

It is definitely worthwhile to extend the trip a little beyond the lake, as long as you avoid venturing into avalanche terrain. Snowshoe to the south end of the lake and continue going south, through light trees, staying toward the left side of the valley. Although steep slopes start to rear up on either side of you, the mature trees in the valley bottom show that in general avalanches do not reach this area.

Directions

The terrain soon opens up and now you will see several obvious avalanche slopes coming down from Commonwealth Ridge to your left. This will be the end of the line for you if you do not have avalanche training. Take in the scenery and return the way you came.

If you do have avalanche training, and feel confident that continuing on is safe, you can reduce the risk by going over to the right side of the valley, but this by no means will put you in a completely safe place. Continue up the valley. If you turn around you will see the familiar forms of Mount Nestor and Old Goat Mountain towering above Spray Lake.

When you start to see large boulders to your right, turn in that direction, gain some elevation and make your way up and over to them. Here the scene really opens up: numerous huge boulders strewn across the landscape, steep, snow-covered slopes all around and Commonwealth Peak standing proudly above the whole scene. On a clear day the adjective "breathtaking" won't do it justice!

The continuation of this trip to Pig's Back is an advanced snowshoeing route, described in the second edition of *Snowshoeing in the Canadian Rockies*. Return the same way to the lake. Remember that once back at the lake, there are two options for descent.

12 Chester Lake

Chester Lake is without question the most popular snowshoeing destination in Kananaskis. The lake is reached via a good snowshoe trail and is surrounded by spectacular mountains. Due to the sheer volume of skiers, snowboarders and snowshoers making their way to Chester Lake, it is imperative that snowshoers use the official snowshoe trail and avoid the ski trail, except on those few short sections where the trail is shared.

DIFFICULTY: advanced
ELEVATION GAIN: 310 m
ROUND-TRIP DISTANCE: 8 km
ROUND-TRIP TIME: 3–5 hours
MAPS: 82 J/14 Spray Lakes Reservoir, Gem Trek Kananaskis Lakes

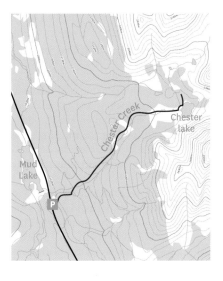

Directions

Drive 6.3 km south of the Engadine Lodge turnoff or 6.2 km north of the Sawmill turnoff and turn east into the Chester Lake parking lot.

The first 400 m of the snowshoe trail is shared with the ski trail. It starts at the north end of the parking lot. Follow the trail for a short distance and take the left fork at the first intersection (well signed). After going over a bridge, look for the snowshoe-trail sign on your right. Turn right onto this trail and follow it through forest and open areas to the beautiful environs of Chester Lake. There are trail signs on trees throughout to guide you. This trail gets very well packed down, and although some will opt to carry their snowshoes on their backpacks, I recommend that you wear snowshoes throughout. Your snowshoe crampons will make the steep sections easy on ascent and descent.

Detour to Elephant Rocks

If you have made it to Chester Lake, a quick detour to Elephant Rocks is almost mandatory. The small amount of elevation that you must gain in the trip to the rocks allows the views to open up a fair amount, and the rocks themselves are fascinating. The turnoff for the valley is a few hundred metres along the northwest shore of Chester Lake. Turn left and snowshoe in a northwesterly direction, arriving at Elephant Rocks in short order.

ABOVE: *The magnificent environs around Chester Lake. Views like this explain the popularity of the area.*

BELOW: *Some of the outstanding views en route to the lake. Chester Lake is not visible but lies to the right of the photo. LG=Little Galatea. MG=Mount Galatea. GP=Gusty Peak. (Jack Tannett)*

ABOVE: *Matthew Clay and Sandra Jacques at Chester Lake. The prominent peak to the left is the southwest end of Gusty Peak, and The Fortress sits in the distant centre. (Matthew Clay)*

BELOW: *Sometimes, in favour of the grand views, we forget to notice the small stuff. Matthew Clay beautifully captures the exquisite detail of frozen water near the lake. (Matthew Clay)*

Nicole Lisafeld enjoying the striking scenery at Elephant Rocks.

13 Lower Chester Loop and Mount Murray Viewpoint

On this trip you won't enjoy the same kind of outstanding scenery as you would experience at Chester Lake, but this loop makes for a relatively short and easy day. Likely, the traffic around the loop will be a fraction of the line of snowshoers and skiers making their way to the lake. The loop can be done in either direction, but clockwise is a little easier in regards to finding the route and is the direction described below. If you are blessed with clear skies, the extension to the Mount Murray Viewpoint is worth the extra effort, but again, don't expect the views to knock you off your snowshoes!

DIFFICULTY: easy

ELEVATION GAIN: 70 m for the loop; add 130 m for the viewpoint

ROUND-TRIP DISTANCE: 4.4 km for the loop; add 2.4 km for the viewpoint

ROUND-TRIP TIME: 1–2.5 hours

MAPS: 82 J/14 Spray Lakes Reservoir, Gem Trek Kananaskis Lakes

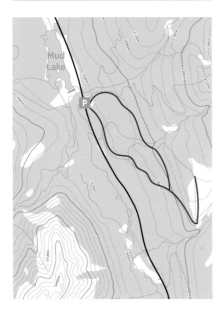

Directions

Drive 6.3 km south of the Engadine Lodge turnoff or 6.2 km north of the Sawmill turnoff and turn east into the Chester Lake parking lot.

From the parking lot follow the normal route to Chester Lake for about 100 m until the trail splits at a major and well-signed junction. Take the right fork and follow it for about 700 m to another junction. This one is unsigned. One fork goes to the left (northeast) up a fairly steep-looking hill. Take the right fork. Snowshoe another 1.4 km to the signed southeast end of the loop.

If you are only doing the loop, take a sharp right and head downhill to complete the loop. The only place where you might encounter a route-finding issue is a sharp turn to the right as you cross a creek a few hundred metres from the parking lot. You'll emerge from the forest at the opposite end of the parking lot from which you departed.

Extension to Mount Murray Viewpoint

Directions

Even if you don't go all the way to the Mount Murray Viewpoint, the 600-m trek to the next major

ABOVE: *The path up to the viewpoint lies at the left. Mount Chester at the right. (Jack Tannett)*
BELOW: *A zoomed-in photo of the east face of Mount Birdwood. (Jack Tannett)*

junction provides a decent view – perhaps even better than one from the viewpoint. Along the way, there are a few brief views to enjoy of the steep east face of Mount Murray. At the signed junction, the scenery opens up quite a bit, especially to the northeast. On a clear day the views of Mount Chester are very pleasant.

An additional 600 m and about 70 m of elevation are required to finish the job. The obvious trail heads up to the viewpoint in a northwesterly direction. An orange snowshoe sign directs you to turn west (left) for the final 50 m. The viewpoint sits amid a fair number of trees, so some walking about is required to get all the views. In terms of spectacular vantage points, it's not exactly the Canadian equivalent of the summit of Everest, so try not to be disappointed! Nevertheless, a good camera will be able to capture some good, zoomed-in shots of Mount Murray, Mount Birdwood, Commonwealth Peak and Mount Chester. Return the same way when you tire of the "walkabout." For variety, the lower leg of the Lower Chester Loop, as described above, is recommended.

14 Hogarth Lakes

The area around Hogarth and Mud lakes is a great route for beginners to get acquainted with snowshoeing in Kananaskis. The loop route has a negligible amount of elevation gain and there are infinite opportunities for exploring, should you feel like leaving the beaten path.

DIFFICULTY: easy
ELEVATION GAIN: minimal
ROUND-TRIP DISTANCE: 4.5-km loop
ROUND-TRIP TIME: 1.5–2.5 hours
MAPS: 82 J/14 Spray Lakes Reservoir, Gem Trek Kananaskis Lakes

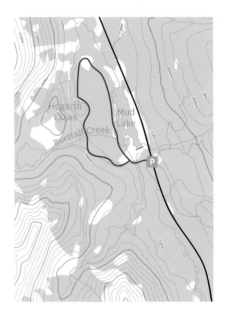

Directions

Drive 6.3 km south of the Engadine Lodge turnoff or 6.2 km north of the Sawmill turnoff and turn west into the Burstall Pass parking lot.

Snowshoe the common trail southwest for 100 m or so, looking for the first orange snowshoe marker on the right side. Once you've found it, simply follow the markers as they take you west and then northwest toward Hogarth Lakes. For those who want to experience the joys (?) of trail-breaking, leave the well-trodden path at any time to do some exploring.

The markers take you to the northeast end of Hogarth Lakes in about 2 km. At this point, the official trail turns south, following the east edge of both Hogarth Lakes. Follow the trail, as it heads in easterly and southerly directions back to Burstall Pass Trail, a few hundred metres from where you left the main trail initially.

Above: *Nicole Lisafeld wades through deep snow south of Mud Lake. The route to Hogarth Lakes lies to the left.*

BELOW: *The official start of the Hogarth Lakes Loop. Mount Birdwood, Commonwealth Peak and Commonwealth Ridge provide an excellent backdrop.*

15 Burstall Lakes

The strategic location of this string of lakes makes it an ideal destination to see some great mountain scenery. Clear skies will reward those who make the trip. You should have excellent views of peaks of the Spray Range, including the awesome south sides of Mount Birdwood, Pig's Tail and Commonwealth Peak.

DIFFICULTY: easy

ELEVATION GAIN: approximately 100 m

ROUND-TRIP DISTANCE: 10 km

ROUND-TRIP TIME: 3–5 hours

MAPS: 82 J/14 Spray Lakes Reservoir, Gem Trek Kananaskis Lakes

Directions

Drive 6.3 km south of the Engadine Lodge turnoff or 6.2 km north of the Sawmill turnoff and turn west into the Burstall Pass parking lot.

From the north end of the parking lot, snowshoe southwest on the obvious trail past Mud Lake and the turnoff to Hogarth Lakes. You are on the Burstall Pass hiking trail, and in winter this is a very popular route for snowshoers and skiers. It is imperative that you do not snowshoe on any

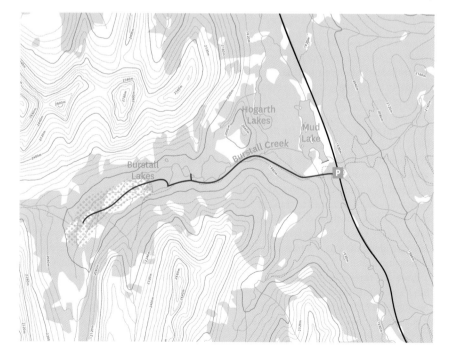

Break time near Burstall Lakes. Michelle and Nicole enjoy a rest and the magnificent scenery. Mount Robertson is the pointy peak at the left, Sir Douglas sits to the right and Robertson Glacier separates them.

ski tracks. The path is wide and there is plenty of room for everyone. If no snowshoe trail exists when you get there, you and your party have been granted the honour of breaking one!

Ignore the snowshoe signs as you continue southwest. The trail turns south (left), ascending a small hill, and then curves around to the west (right). French Creek Trail stems off at this point, heading southeast. Ignore that trail too, and continue following Burstall Pass trail, at first west and then southwest. Although the trail is never steep, it does gain and lose elevation along the way. Prepare for a little huffing and puffing.

There are three Burstall Lakes, and although you can certainly visit all three, the suggested route makes a quick stop at the second and then goes right to the third and most westerly lake. Snowshoe the Burstall Pass trail for about 35–50 minutes (approximately 2 km from the parking lot). Start looking for a fairly obvious path to your right (north). That path leads very quickly to the second lake and is worth a quick look. The lake is surrounded on all sides by trees but has good views of the southeast sides of Commonwealth Peak and Mount Birdwood.

Return to the main trail and snowshoe another 400–500 m, where another path breaks off to the north. This one goes to the third lake and a wide-open view of the area. This is a great place to take a lunch break and absorb the excellent views. After fuelling up on both, you can return to the parking lot the same way you came in or continue southwest for even better views. If you do decide to call it a day, don't try

Nicole and Snow Peak. No cell reception yet, but wait a few years!

any alternative routes back. You may end up below avalanche slopes and/or on very steep and dangerous terrain.

Hopefully, you and your party have decided to continue southwest for approximately 1 km. The impressively long ridge in front of you and to your left (southwest) is called Whistling Rock Ridge and it terminates in a magnificently statuesque pile of Rockies rubble called Mount Sir Douglas – the 34th highest mountain in the Canadian Rockies. As you snowshoe southwest, this terrific mountain will come into view, as well as Robertson Glacier and an even more striking (but lower) mountain to the east of the glacier, named Mount Robertson. Don't stop until you can see Robertson – it will be worth it. Throughout, the views of Birdwood, Pig's Tail and Commonwealth continue to change and improve.

You can take your second break of the day when Robertson appears. Travel beyond this point is possible but not recommended. The trail goes west, up and through trees into the upper valley. Eventually you end up in avalanche terrain near Burstall Pass. While the scenery here is fantastic, you should not approach this area without avalanche training and gear. Stick to the lower valley, where there should be enough to ogle at for some time, and then return the same way you came in. Again, don't try any alternative routes or shortcuts.

16 Sawmill Trails

*The snowshoe trails starting from the Sawmill parking lot have been under development for the past few years but are finally complete. All are terrific beginner routes though lacking in great views. They provide good exercise and the option for many variations, as well as access to more scenic areas, such as "James Walker Lake" (page 94) and the Kent Ridge outlier (*Snowshoeing in the Canadian Rockies*, 2nd Edition).*

Hardcore shoers can go all the way to the Chester Lake parking lot, via Sawmill Loop, Snowdrift and the upper leg of Frost Heave and then return via the lower leg of Frost Heave and Graupel. That would entail approximately 20 km of snowshoeing, with about 500 m of elevation gain, and would take up the better part of a day. Another option, if two vehicles are available, is to make a one-way trip via one of those routes and then drive back to the Sawmill parking lot.

A beautiful day on the Sawmill Loop. (Matthew Clay)

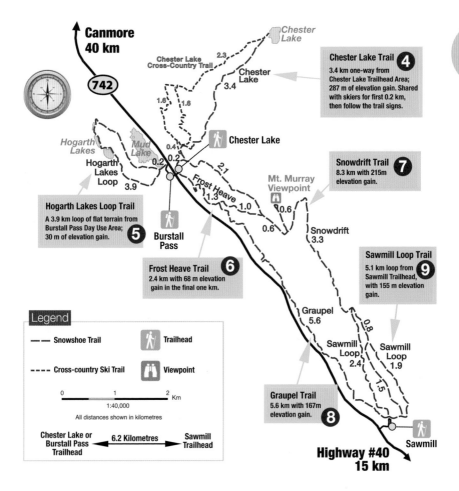

Canmore
40 km

742

Chester Lake
Cross-Country Trail

2.3

Chester
Lake

Chester
Lake
3.4

1.6   1.6

Chester Lake Trail 4
3.4 km one-way from
Chester Lake Trailhead Area;
287 m of elevation gain. Shared
with skiers for first 0.2 km,
then follow the trail signs.

Hogarth
Lakes

Mud
Lake

Chester Lake

0.4
0.2   0.2

Hogarth
Lakes
Loop   3.9

2.1

Mt. Murray
Viewpoint

Snowdrift Trail 7
8.3 km with 215m
elevation gain.

Frost Heave
1.3   1.0

0.6

Hogarth Lakes Loop Trail
A 3.9 km loop of flat terrain from
Burstall Pass Day Use Area;
30 m of elevation gain. **5**

Burstall
Pass

0.6

Snowdrift
3.3

Sawmill Loop Trail
5.1 km loop from
Sawmill Trailhead,
with 155 m elevation
gain. **9**

Frost Heave Trail 6
2.4 km with 68 m elevation
gain in the final one km.

Graupel
5.6

0.8

Legend

Sawmill
Loop
2.4

Sawmill
Loop
1.9

—— Snowshoe Trail   Trailhead

- - - Cross-country Ski Trail   Viewpoint

0   1   2
                              Km
1:40,000
All distances shown in kilometres

1.5

Graupel Trail
5.6 km with 167m
elevation gain. **8**

Sawmill

Chester Lake or   6.2 Kilometres   Sawmill
Burstall Pass   ◄————————►   Trailhead
Trailhead

Highway #40
15 km

The official snowshoe trails around Chester Lake, Hogarth Lakes, and the Sawmill area, with distances and elevation gains (map courtesy of Alberta Parks, Kananaskis).

17 "James Walker Lake"

For those craving a little more challenge and far superior scenery than that offered by the Sawmill trails, this small but picturesque lake is a terrific destination. A well-used summer trail takes you into the heart of one of the stunning hanging valleys of the Kananaskis Range. The lake appears to lack an official name, but given it's the largest body of water that feeds James Walker Creek, the title "James Walker Lake" seems appropriate.

DIFFICULTY: intermediate

ELEVATION GAIN: approximately 260 m

ROUND-TRIP DISTANCE: 8.5 km

ROUND-TRIP TIME: 3–5 hours

MAPS: 82 J/14 Spray Lakes Reservoir, 82 J/11 Kananaskis Lakes, Gem Trek Kananaskis Lakes

Directions

Park at the Sawmill parking lot near the south end of Highway 742. There are several snowshoe trails that leave the lot – take the one behind the outhouse, heading east and uphill. Within minutes you'll reach a signed fork in the trail. Take the left fork, labelled as the "1.5" section. The "1.9" section to the right can also be used but adds 400 m to the trip. Follow either path to where they intersect. From the intersection, continue in a northwesterly direction for about 350–400 m, looking for an unsigned and narrower trail that branches off to the right and goes uphill (GR233250). There is an identical-looking trail doing exactly the same thing a few hundred metres before – ignore that one.

You are now on the unofficial "James Walker Lake" trail. Following this trail takes you directly to the lake. The trail is narrow but obvious and more or less goes in long straight lines. Trail-breaking may be quite strenuous if you are the first to do so. Although you are surrounded by trees, good views of the impressive unnamed peak to the north are soon plentiful.

Eventually the straight trail gives way to a more winding path as it heads into the trees. The trail is a little harder to follow, but occasional flagging in the trees helps. In short order a boulder field appears to the left. Here you can stay on the trail, circumventing the field on the right side or go exploring right through this fascinating field of rock (highly recommended). Mount James Walker soon appears at the end of the valley, with the steep walls of Mount

ABOVE: *The superb scenery near the lake. Part of the boulder field in the foreground, an unnamed peak to the left, Mount James Walker at the distant centre and Mount Inflexible to the right.*

BELOW: *To the west sit Mount Murray (centre) and unofficial "Cegnfs" (right).*

Inflexible towering over the right side of the valley.

Continue working your way through the boulder field or around it, eventually ending up at the south end of "James Walker Lake." You can snowshoe around the lake, but views don't really improve. Instead, take in the wonderful views from the south end and then return the same way. In case you were thinking of going farther, the slopes beyond the lake put you in serious avalanche terrain (highly unadvisable unless you are properly equipped).

18 Warspite Lake

This is a popular trip that is perfect for beginners. The view at Warspite Lake is decent, but going just a little past the lake really opens things up with terrific views of massive Mount Black Prince. Beyond that, you are getting into avalanche terrain, so go no farther.

DIFFICULTY: easy

ELEVATION GAIN: 120 m

ROUND-TRIP DISTANCE: 4 km

ROUND-TRIP TIME: 2–4 hours

MAPS: 82 J/11 Kananaskis Lakes, Gem Trek Kananaskis Lakes

Directions

Park at the Black Prince parking lot, near the south end of Highway 742.

The interpretive trail follows Smith–Dorrien Creek for about 100 m, crosses the creek and then turns back along the creek, before veering off to the right. It is well marked and easy to follow. In winter there is often a small shortcut to the left, near the parking lot, that crosses the creek over a snow bridge. Late in the season this bridge will be either gone or dicey – best to follow the summer trail in that case.

Both trails quickly unite and then a long uphill grind starts, heading to the right (northwest). The slope is not terribly steep and travel will be easy. Expect to see skiers and ski tracks along the way. Stay off the ski tracks.

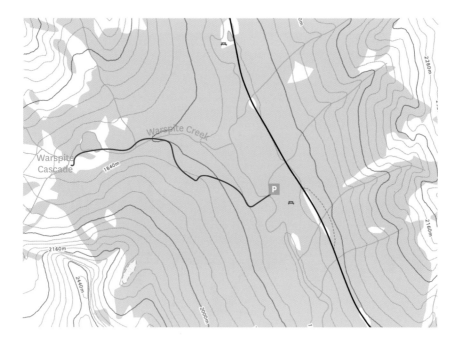

ABOVE: *That crazy Calgary Stampeder fan from Crandell Lake turns up at Warspite Lake – 250 km north – very eerie!*

Below: *The view from beyond Warspite Lake, with the route to Warspite Cirque. Not sure what the Stampeder fan is doing.*

At the top of the hill the trail seems to swing around to the left (southwest), but the route to the lake takes the less obvious right fork, where a bench sits (probably partially or completely submerged in snow). Stay right and keep following the trail as you lose a chunk of the elevation you just gained. When the terrain levels out, the trail veers slightly to the left, eventually crossing a creek and then heading left again and gently uphill to the lake. There could be a multitude of other ski and snowshoe trails – it's best to just follow the most prominent one.

The actual lake is more like a big puddle and may fail to impress. Of more interest is the intriguing form of Mount Black Prince, looming above the lake. To the left of the lake, an advanced snowshoeing trip continues on to Warspite Cirque. It is definitely worth your while to wander over to the southwest side of the lake and through a small stand of trees. Beyond the trees the scenery opens up again to some beautiful vistas. Much of the steep route to Warspite Cirque is visible and, due to steepness, should make everyone shudder just a little! Travelling farther up the valley will bring you into avalanche terrain. Turn around and return the same way you came in.

Kananaskis Lakes Trail

Many of the routes along Kananaskis Lakes Trail centre on the amazing Lower and Upper Kananaskis Lakes. Snow depths here can exceed 2 m and may persist well into April and even early May. Like Highway 742, you are almost guaranteed to have good, deep snow to snowshoe on or through from January to mid-April.

The weather can be quite finicky in this area of the Rockies. It is not uncommon for murky, whiteout-like conditions to exist around the lakes, while sunny (or at least sunnier) skies prevail farther north, northeast and east.

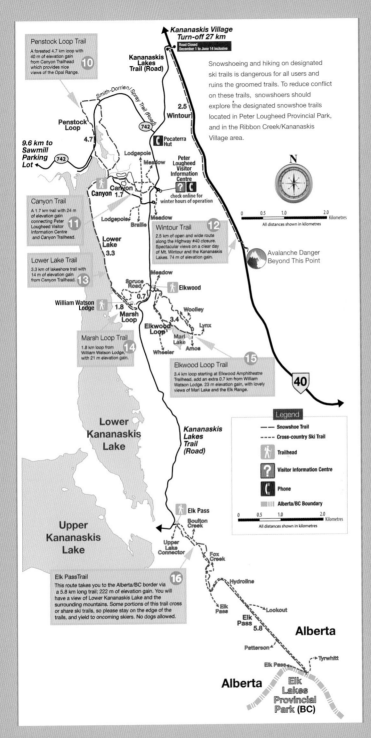

The official snowshoe trails around the Kananaskis Lakes (map courtesy of Alberta Parks, Kananaskis).

Kananaskis Village Turn-off 27 km
Road Closed December 1 to June 14 inclusive

Kananaskis Lakes Trail (Road)

Penstock Loop Trail
A forested 4.7 km loop with 40 m of elevation gain from Canyon Trailhead which provides nice views of the Opal Range.
10

Smith-Dorrien / Spray Trail (Road)

Penstock Loop
4.7

742

2.5 Wintour

Pocaterra Hut

9.6 km to Sawmill Parking Lot
742

Snowshoeing and hiking on designated ski trails is dangerous for all users and ruins the groomed trails. To reduce conflict on these trails, snowshoers should explore the designated snowshoe trails located in Peter Lougheed Provincial Park, and in the Ribbon Creek/Kananaskis Village area.

Lodgepole
Meadow

Peter Lougheed Visitor Information Centre
check online for winter hours of operation

N

Canyon Trail
A 1.7 km trail with 24 m of elevation gain connecting Peter Lougheed Visitor Information Centre and Canyon Trailhead.
11

Canyon 1.7

Lodgepole
Braille
Meadow

0 0.5 1.0 2.0 Kilometres
All distances shown in kilometres

Wintour Trail
2.5 km of open and wide route along the Highway #40 closure. Spectacular views on a clear day of Mt. Wintour and the Kananaskis Lakes. 74 m of elevation gain.
12

Lower Lake
3.3

Lower Lake Trail
3.3 km of lakeshore trail with 14 m of elevation gain from Canyon Trailhead.
13

Avalanche Danger Beyond This Point

Meadow

Spruce Road
0.7
Elkwood

William Watson Lodge
1.8
Marsh Loop

Woolley

Elkwood Loop
3.4
Lynx

Marsh Loop Trail
1.8 km loop from William Watson Lodge, with 21 m of elevation gain.
14

Marl Lake
Amos
Wheeler

Elkwood Loop Trail
3.4 km loop starting at Elkwood Amphitheatre Trailhead, add an extra 0.7 km from William Watson Lodge. 23 m elevation gain, with lovely views of Marl Lake and the Elk Range.
15

40

Lower Kananaskis Lake

Kananaskis Lakes Trail (Road)

Legend
— Snowshoe Trail
--- Cross-country Ski Trail
Trailhead
? Visitor Information Centre
Phone
|||| Alberta/BC Boundary

0 0.5 1.0 2.0 Kilometres
All distances shown in kilometres

Upper Kananaskis Lake

Elk Pass
Boulton Creek
Upper Lake Connector
Fox Creek

Elk Pass Trail
This route takes you to the Alberta/BC border via a 5.8 km long trail; 222 m of elevation gain. You will have a view of Lower Kananaskis Lake and the surrounding mountains. Some portions of this trail cross or share ski trails, so please stay on the edge of the trails, and yield to oncoming skiers. No dogs allowed.
16

Hydroline
Elk Pass
Lookout
Elk Pass 5.8

Patterson
Tyrwhitt

Alberta

Elk Pass

Alberta
Elk Lakes Provincial Park (BC)

Nina and the view of Lower Kananaskis Lake from near Upper Kananaskis Lake. The magnificent Opal Range always provides a fantastic background.

19 Lower Kananaskis Lake I

The Lower Lake snowshoe trail is just the summer trail, but with snow. Expansive views are available from beginning to end.

DIFFICULTY: easy

ELEVATION GAIN: approximately 30 m

ROUND-TRIP DISTANCE: 5.6 km

ROUND-TRIP TIME: 1.5–2.5 hours

MAPS: 82 J/11 Kananaskis Lakes, Gem Trek Kananaskis Lakes

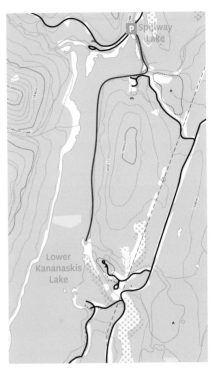

Directions

Drive 3.9 km along Kananaskis Lakes Trail and turn onto the Canyon road. Follow it to the parking lot.

There are three ways to snowshoe this route: along the designated trail, on the embankment above the lake, or directly on the lake. Provided there is good snow coverage, I recommend using the embankment on the way in and following the designated trail on the way back or vice versa. Your decision regarding which route to start with may depend on the weather. The embankment route has better views and therefore favours good weather. Both routes are described below.

Lower Lake Trail Route

This route starts at the trailhead sign and is clearly marked with an orange snowshoe sign. The popularity of the trail means that it will probably be packed down and very easy to follow. The trail goes through the trees, staying relatively close to the lakeshore for the first half and then moving very close to the shore for the second half. Views of the lake and its surroundings are obviously better on the second half of the trip.

The trail ends at an obvious peninsula with a small brown building at the end.

This is also the north end of the Marsh Loop. Time, energy and motivation permitting, you may want to complete the 1.8-km Marsh Loop and then return via Lower Lake Trail or the embankment.

Embankment Route

This route is perhaps even easier to follow than the designated trail. From the parking lot snowshoe a few metres north onto the bank of Lower Lake. Head west and then curve around to the south, staying above the lake. Views toward the Opal Range to the northeast are fantastic right off the

ABOVE: *The rewards of the embankment route are instant views of the Opal Range …*

BELOW: *…and the Battle of Jutland group.*

A late-season trip reveals large fractures and fissures in the ice on the embankment. A week earlier these cracks were all filled in with a weak layer of snow. Take care.

bat, as are views toward Mount Warspite due west. Rounding the corner, Invincible and Indefatigable soon appear and finally Sarrail, Foch and Fox in the distant south.

Take extreme care if at any time you decide to descend to the lake. Deep snow can hide large cracks and holes in the broken slabs of thick ice that often line the lakeshore.

Continue following the lake south for several kilometres. Your goal is to snowshoe to the small brown building at the end of a peninsula and then follow the peninsula east to the designated trail (snowshoe sign to the left). The snowshoe sign to the right is for the north end of the 1.8-km Marsh Loop, and you may want to complete that short trip while in the area (page 116).

For return, either retrace your steps along the embankment, or, for a little variety, follow the designated trail back to the parking lot. The gentle ups and downs of the trail make this a very pleasant route to take.

20 Elk Pass

The Elk Pass snowshoe trail is a good day of exercise, but not much else. Views are limited throughout and at the pass there is hardly a view at all. However, the trail can be used as an approach to Kananaskis Lookout or Fox Lake. You can also make a pleasant loop route by going to Elk Pass via the snowshoe trail and then returning via Fox Creek. This area is used often by skiers so please respect their space and tracks.

DIFFICULTY: intermediate

PASS HEIGHT: 1950 m

NET ELEVATION GAIN: 222 m

ROUND-TRIP DISTANCE: 11.6-12.4 km

ROUND-TRIP TIME: 3–5 hours

MAPS: 82 J/11 Kananaskis Lakes, Gem Trek Kananaskis Lakes

Directions

Drive approximately 12 km on Kananaskis Trail and park at the Elk Pass parking lot. The snowshoe trail starts at the southeast end of the parking lot. It very quickly empties out onto the wide Hydroline ski trail. From here the official snowshoe trail is well signed and easy to follow. A detailed description is not required, however a few pointers may help.

The trail ascends to the top of the first hill, going into the trees a couple of times along the way. First on the right side of the Hydroline and then on the left. Continue up until you arrive at a point where the trail overlooks a deep canyon, with a continuation of the Hydroline far on the other side. The snowshoe trail now joins up with the ski trail and descends to the bottom of the valley. Stay to the side of the path and watch for skiers. At the bottom, the trail turns left and then takes an immediate right into the trees, where it parallels Fox Creek, before popping out back onto the ski trail.

Turn left and ascend a long gentle slope back up to the Hydroline. At the top you may want to quickly veer off to the left to take in a pretty decent view of Kananaskis Lakes and Mount Indefatigable.

The remainder of the trip involves a somewhat mundane plod to Elk Pass along the Hydroline. Don't expect any mind-blowing views on the way or at the pass.

Otherwise, continue up to the high point of Elk Pass, around GR367055. An "End of the Trail" sign marks the end of the ascent.

For return you can retrace your steps back or complete a loop route via Elk Pass Trail. This second option is recommended, but note that this means you will be on a ski trail for a large section. Stay to the side and yield to all skiers throughout. The route is again obvious.

Hop onto Elk Pass Trail and descend easily to the valley below. Consider a side trip to Fox Lake at this point (see page 109). Eventually the trail joins up with Fox Creek and parallels it for a while. This is probably the most pleasant part of the trip, with terrific scenery along and in the creek.

About 4.4 km from the high point at Elk Pass, Elk Pass Trail joins up with Hydroline trail. The remainder of the trip is the same as what you ascended.

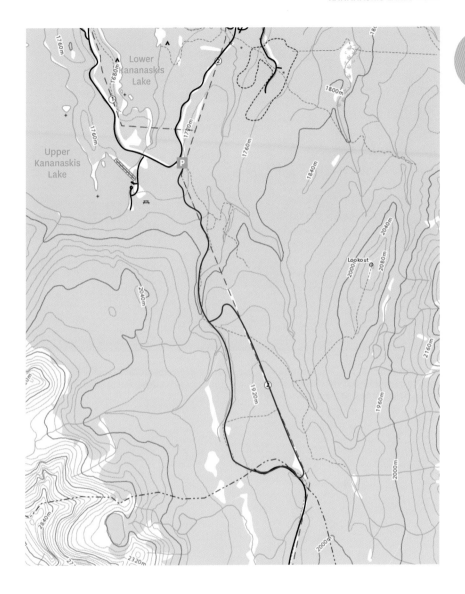

The Dewit family, Kaycie, Hanneke and Niko, ascend the wide Hydroline. Note that the family is making a separate snowshoe trail alongside the ski trail – kudos to them! Mount Indefatigable basks in the sun behind them. (Vern Dewit)

21 Fox Lake

As with many winter visits to lakes, the highlight of this trip is not the actual lake. Fox Lake in winter is usually a white, frozen flatland and far more interesting in the summer. The winter reward is the journey there and the view of Mount Fox above the lake. The recommended route is a loop using the Elk Pass snowshoe trail on ascent and Fox Creek for return.

DIFFICULTY: intermediate

LAKE HEIGHT: 1950 m

NET ELEVATION GAIN: 300 m (via Elk Pass)

ROUND-TRIP DISTANCE: 14.4 km (via Elk Pass)

ROUND-TRIP TIME: 4–7 hours

MAPS: 82 J/11 Kananaskis Lakes, Gem Trek Kananaskis Lakes

Directions

Follow the directions to Elk Pass. From the pass hop onto Elk Pass Trail and descend to the valley below. This is an easy and pleasant descent on skis or snowshoes.

As you near the bottom of the hill, look for a "More Difficult" blue ski sign. Here you will take a sharp left turn onto the summer trail that leads to a major junction. Snowshoe southeast for about 300 m, soon

At the clearing and looking west toward the large sign and stunning Mount Fox. LS=large sign. F=Mount Fox.

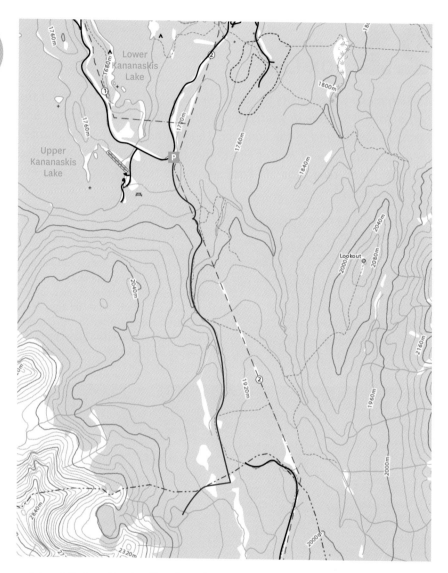

arriving at the large clearing. Even here the view of Mount Fox is quite eye-catching.

On the west side of the clearing you should see a large sign. Make your way over to it. The trail to Fox Lake is well signed (hopefully the sign is not completely buried in snow) and it heads west.

Follow the trail for 200 m to another sign, where you will take a 90° turn left onto another trail. This trail goes through the trees and then empties out into more open terrain. Going straight at this intersection leads to Frozen Lake, but it's a steep grind to get there and certainly not recommended as a winter trip. Visit Frozen Lake in the summer – the view is spectacular!

Route-finding may get a little tricky here, depending on whether a trail to the lake

Andra MacKnight captures the serene beauty of Fox Lake, the snow-covered trees at the back of the lake and the magnificent form of Mount Fox behind the lake. (Andra MacKnight)

has already been broken or not. The goal is to find the creek that drains Fox Lake and follow it on its right bank to the lake (Elkan Creek). Head to the right and up. Eventually you will run into the creek. If not, start trending left as you slowly gain elevation. If that doesn't work, set your GPS to GR354045 to guide you to the lake. If you don't have any form of technology to assist you, it may be time to pray for directions!

Once you have located the creek, simply follow it for several hundred metres to Fox Lake. Take in the view of Mount Fox and then start returning the same way. When you get back to the blue ski sign, turn left back onto Elk Pass Trail. You can now follow this trail, paralleling Fox Creek, all the way back to the Elk Pass snowshoe trail. Rejoin the snowshoe trail and return to the parking lot. Climbing back up the big hill is not as strenuous as you are probably dreading, and then it's a smooth sail downhill all the way back.

22 Penstock Loop

"A forested 4.5 km loop from Canyon Day Use which takes in some interesting historical features, such as the Pocaterra Dam penstock and the Kent Creek sluiceway, and provides nice views of the Opal Range." Thus reads the billing on the Kananaskis Country Snowshoe Trails pamphlet. This loop has a bit of everything, including two road crossings, so be alert. Note that changes were made to this area in spring of 2012 and the described route may change in the future. Check at the Peter Lougheed Visitor Centre before going out.

DIFFICULTY: easy

ELEVATION GAIN: 40 m

ROUND-TRIP DISTANCE: 4.7 km

ROUND-TRIP TIME: 1.5–2.5 hours

MAPS: 82 J/11 Kananaskis Lakes, Gem Trek Kananaskis Lakes

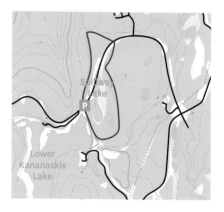

Directions

Drive 3.9 km along Kananaskis Lakes Trail and turn onto the Canyon road. Follow it to the parking lot.

From the parking lot the first snowshoe sign can be found near the northeast end, close to the lake. This is also the start of the canyon trail. The loop can be completed in either direction. Clockwise is described below. Snowshoe east for a short distance and then turn north, crossing the dam. Follow the wide path to the north end of Lower Kananaskis Lake. From there, carefully (and quickly) cross Highway 742, looking for an orange snowshoe sign on the other side.

It is now simply a matter of following the obvious path and signs, first alongside the Kent Creek sluiceway, then into a heavily forested area. The path soon turns east and then south before crossing the highway

again. Good views of the Opal Range appear occasionally.

The loop ends at the huge leaky pipe that each year turns into a sculpture of fascinating ice formations.

ABOVE: *An orderly line of snowshoers enjoy the easy trail.*

BELOW: *Cool ice formations caused by the leaky pipe. (Marko Stavric)*

When you come from a country with little to no snow, adapting to snowshoes may be challenging at first. Uncle Bill from England keeps the troops entertained by demonstrating solid form in falling!

23 Elkwood Loop

The Elkwood Loop takes you through pleasant forest to scenic Marl Lake, where good views of Mount Indefatigable await. The loop can be completed in either direction, but clockwise seems to be the preferred choice and is described below. For a fuller day, the route can easily be combined with the Marsh Loop via the William Watson Connector.

DIFFICULTY: easy

ELEVATION GAIN: 23 m

ROUND-TRIP DISTANCE: 3.4 km

ROUND-TRIP TIME: 45–90 minutes

MAPS: 82 J/11 Kananaskis Lakes,
Gem Trek Kananaskis Lakes

Directions

Drive 5.8 km along Kananaskis Lakes Trail and pull into the Elkwood Amphitheatre parking lot.

Locate the first orange snowshoe sign and snowshoe a short connector to an important three-way junction. Turn left (Elkwood Loop) and follow the snowshoe signs through the campground and sections of forested terrain to the start of Marl Lake Interpretive Trail, about 15 minutes from the parking lot.

The interpretive trail is easy to follow and, provided they are not buried under snow, the interpretive signs are interesting and offer good points to stop and enjoy the scenery. Several open areas give views of small sections of the Opal Range to the east.

When you reach Marl Lake the views open up even more, with a good look at Mount Indefatigable. Those who have ventured up into the Aster Lake area will recognize Warrior Mountain to the distant left of Indefatigable.

At this point you have the option to

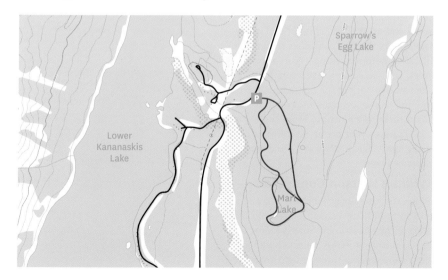

The view of Mount Indefatigable from Marl Lake. (Gillean Daffern)

extend the trip by snowshoeing around the perimeter of the lake. It will add about 1.5 km and 25–40 minutes to the overall trip, but the additional views will reward those who make the effort. This is an extension you'll want to do in late winter or early spring, when snow coverage and ice conditions are usually safe.

Whether you do the extension or not, you'll end up at the northwest end of the lake, where the trail continues for a short distance before turning right, into the trees, up a steep and very short hill. You then emerge back in the campground. Follow the snowshoe signs back to the Elkwood three-way junction. From there you can return to your car or extend your day using the William Watson Connector, as described below.

William Watson Connector

From the three-way junction it's about 700 m to William Watson Lodge and the start of the Marsh Loop. Simply follow the signs, quickly crossing the main road and then snowshoeing through light forest to the lodge. If the trail is packed down, you may want to do this connector on foot, carrying your snowshoes. Otherwise, it will entail a couple of short sections of walking on concrete – never a good idea for the health of your snowshoes! The signed trailhead for the Marsh Loop is to the right (north) of the main lodge.

24 Lower Kananaskis Lake II

For those wanting to avoid the potential crowds along Lower Kananaskis Lake I trail (page 103), see a slightly different section of Lower Kananaskis Lake and/or engage in some potentially serious trail-breaking, this area is a great alternative to Lower Kananaskis Lake I. The intermediate rating of this trip reflects the fact that there are no official trails in this area and there exists the potential for route-finding and trail-breaking.

DIFFICULTY: intermediate

ELEVATION GAIN: minimal

ROUND-TRIP DISTANCE: variable

ROUND-TRIP TIME: variable

MAPS: 82 J/11 Kananaskis Lakes, Gem Trek Kananaskis Lakes

Directions

Drive 9.7 km along Kananaskis Lakes Trail and turn onto the Lower Lake road. Follow it to the parking lot.

The lake is only a few hundred metres from the parking lot. This is a great opportunity to gain experience breaking new trail

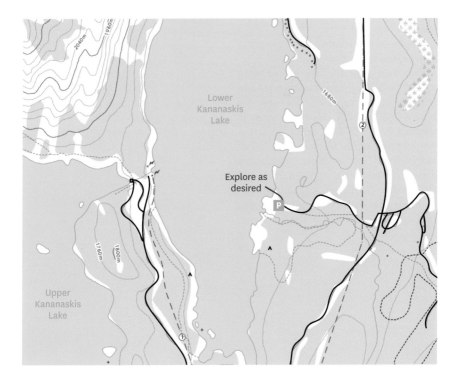

Nina heads out toward the lake. The striking peaks at the left are outliers of Mount Lyautey, and Mount Indefatigable sits to the right.

without too much commitment. It's easy to turn around at any time.

Once near or on the lake, snowshoeing in pretty much any direction will grant you great views of something! Due west lies Mount Indefatigable. Mount Lyautey is the huge massif to the southwest. Farther south sit the familiar forms of Mounts Sarrail, Foch and Fox. The diminutive but very distinctive mountain between Foch and Fox is called The Turret. As you travel farther west on the lake, views of the magnificent Opal Range to the east start to open up.

25 Upper Kananaskis Lake I

If you are looking for great views of Mount Indefatigable, this is the place to see some. The best way to do this is by snowshoeing on the lake, around the south shore. If the lake is not sufficiently frozen, use Rawson Lake Trail. The intermediate rating of this trip reflects the fact that there is potential for route-finding and trail-breaking, unless you stick to the official trails going around the lake.

DIFFICULTY: intermediate
ELEVATION GAIN: minimal
ROUND-TRIP DISTANCE: variable
ROUND-TRIP TIME: variable
MAPS: 82 J/11 Kananaskis Lakes,
Gem Trek Kananaskis Lakes

Directions

Drive 12.4 km along Kananaskis Lakes Trail and turn onto the Upper Lake road. Follow it to the parking lot at the southeast end of Upper Kananaskis Lake.

Either snowshoe immediately down to the shore of the lake as your starting point or follow the obvious trail that goes around the southeast corner of the lake (same as

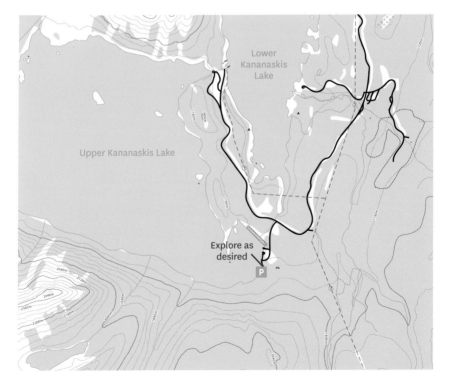

Looking across the lake from the parking lot. Acres and acres of beautiful views and terrain to enjoy. (Greg Stringham)

for Rawson Lake, page 121). When the lake is fully frozen you can explore this area in any direction you like. Going straight into the middle of the lake will be fantastic for views. Following the shoreline in either direction is also a great way to experience this awe-inspiring environment.

26 Rawson Lake

This small lake sits below the awe-inspiring northeast face of Mount Sarrail. A well-used trail goes all the way there. The extension to the ridge north of Rawson Lake grants a great view of the considerably larger Kananaskis Lakes, but it is beyond the scope of this book because of avalanche danger.

DIFFICULTY: intermediate
ELEVATION GAIN: 300 m
ROUND-TRIP DISTANCE: 8 km
ROUND-TRIP TIME: 3–5 hours
MAPS: 82 J/11 Kananaskis Lakes,
Gem Trek Kananaskis Lakes

Directions

Drive 12.4 km along Kananaskis Lakes Trail and turn onto the Upper Lake road. Follow it to the parking lot at the southeast end of Upper Kananaskis Lake.

From there, start along the easy-to-follow trail that swings around the southeast end of Upper Kananaskis Lake and then

Mount Sarrail reflected in the placid waters of Rawson Lake. Probably not a good time to attempt to snowshoe across the lake!

parallels the south side. About 1 km along you'll cross a bridge that spans Sarrail Creek. Shortly after, a trail sign instructs you to leave the main trail and turn left (southwest) onto Rawson Lake Trail. Follow this trail for 2 km as it winds its way up treed slopes to Rawson Lake. Take some time to enjoy the tranquil beauty of this area. Provided the lake is sufficiently frozen, you can snowshoe across it; however, there are avalanche concerns on the opposite side. The best strategy is to follow the perimeter of the lake for short distances in either direction to get some different perspectives. Return the same way you came in.

27 Upper Kananaskis Lake II

The second of two starting points on Upper Lake offers terrific views of massive Mount Lyautey and the Sarrail/Foch/Fox trio. When it is sufficiently frozen, you can snowshoe directly on the lake. If conditions on the lake are suspect, a very popular trail goes around the north side of the lake. For those of you who are goal-oriented, the treed island, sometimes called Hawke Island, in the middle of the lake is a good objective. The intermediate rating of this trip reflects the fact that there is potential for route-finding and trail-breaking, unless you stick to the official trails going around the lake.

DIFFICULTY: intermediate

ELEVATION GAIN: minimal

ROUND-TRIP DISTANCE: variable

ROUND-TRIP TIME: variable

MAPS: 82 J/11 Kananaskis Lakes, Gem Trek Kananaskis Lakes

Directions

Drive 14.7 km along Kananaskis Lakes Trail and turn left onto the North Interlakes road, reaching the parking lot shortly after.

Upper Lake is metres away from the parking lot. Do not jump onto the lake immediately. The release of water at the dam makes this area of the lake very unstable.

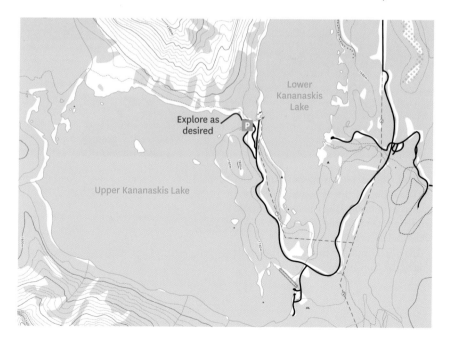

ABOVE: *Upper Kananaskis Lake. The northwest outliers of Mount Lyautey dominate the background. Note the lake area at the front is susceptible to weak ice and should be avoided. (Gary Hebert)*

BELOW: *Mark Koob and son snowshoeing around the Upper Kananaskis Lake. (Tanya Koob)*

Instead, snowshoe northwest, across the initial section of the dam, and then make your way onto the lake when it is feasible (and safe). Once on the lake, it's up to you where and how far you go.

The other option is to stay on the south side of the dam and follow the shore.

Banff

Banff is Canada's classic mountain town. Visitors flock from every corner of the planet throughout the year to see Banff and the national park. Though not as snowy as its equally popular neighbour to the northwest, Lake Louise, Banff gets enough snow to keep the average snowshoer in business for the length of the season. As well, the weather tends to be a little more stable than it is at Lake Louise, due to Banff's more easterly location.

On average, Banff receives its largest deposits of snow in December and January. However, usually the best snowshoeing conditions occur in February and March, when the snowpack has settled and consolidated.

For the most part, finding accommodations in Banff is pretty easy, the townsite being home to a great number of hotels. However, don't expect that to be inexpensive, and book in advance, especially for long weekends.

A national park pass is required for all trips in Banff.

Dramatic uplifts of ice along the Lake Minnewanka shoreline.

28 Lake Minnewanka and Stewart Canyon

You can't go wrong visiting this outstanding lake on a clear day. The scenery on the lake is terrific and the views around the lake are wonderful. Although there is a good trail around the west side of the lake, the best way to enjoy the scenery is by staying very close to the shore. This means some travel on the lake, so be sure it is sufficiently frozen by going in January or February. Extending the trip to include a trek up Stewart Canyon is a good way to get some additional exercise, but the scenery is not as good as that on the lake. Note that Stewart Canyon is an intermediate trip because of short sections where you must travel close to a drop-off.

DIFFICULTY: easy for Lake Minnewanka; intermediate for Stewart Canyon

ELEVATION GAIN: minimal for the lake; approximately 100 m for Stewart Canyon

ROUND-TRIP DISTANCE: 2–6 km

ROUND-TRIP TIME: 0.75–2.5 hours

MAPS: 82 O/03 Canmore, 82 O/06 Lake Minnewanka, Gem Trek Banff and Mount Assiniboine

---

Directions

From the Trans-Canada Highway, take the Lake Minnewanka turnoff near Banff. Drive 9.4 km to the Lake Minnewanka parking lot. Note the winter detour along the way, about 1 km after leaving Highway 1.

From the parking lot, make your way down to the lake and start snowshoeing north along the lakeshore. If the huge uplifts of cracked ice along the shore don't keep you entertained, the immediate views of Inglismaldie and the unnamed peak on the north side of the lake should.

Those who have seen this lake in the summer know full well that in many places the lake bottom simply drops off at the shore,

without a gradual slope. Just another reminder to be sure of the strength of the ice as you make your way around the lake. If at any point travel along the lakeshore seems risky, leave the shore and find the trail to the west.

Go as far as you like before turning around. Some of the most interesting scenery is about 700 m to 1 km along the shore. A good objective that is not too strenuous is to go around the lakeshore until you see a large shelter with a trailhead kiosk behind it. Leaving the lake, you can then take the easy trail back to the parking lot in a very short amount of time. If you want a little more exercise, go to the aforementioned Lake Minnewanka kiosk by the shelter. Snowshoe or hike 800 m farther along the trail to the cool bridge spanning the Cascade River and a pleasant view up Stewart Canyon. Return to the parking lot via the wide trail or continue up Stewart Canyon for some more exercise.

Extension to Stewart Canyon

You'll probably do this extension more for the exercise than the scenery. The terrain is interesting but views are limited. Also,

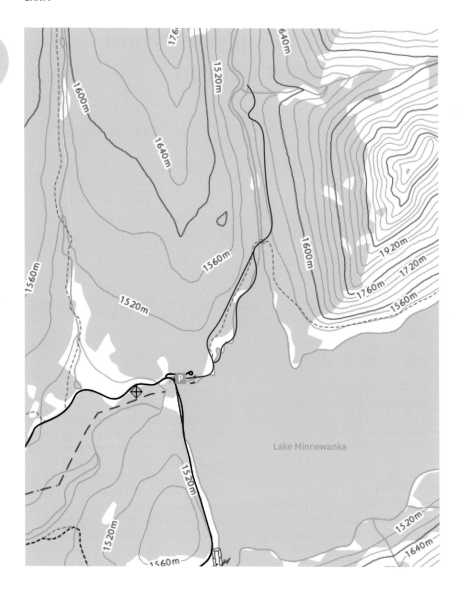

Lake Minnewanka

The unique chemistry and physics of ice – one of the few substances that expands when turning from liquid to solid. Note the large shelter to the left: a good objective for the trip.

through a few sections, the trek up the canyon does follow along the edge of a very steep drop-off into the canyon below. Those not used to such situations may find travel a little unnerving for brief periods.

Directions

From the Lake Minnewanka kiosk by the shelter, snowshoe or hike 800 m farther along the trail to the bridge spanning the Cascade River. Cross the bridge and turn left, continuing on the trail that now parallels the Cascade River but high above it. Approximately 150 m later you'll arrive at a major, signed junction. Take the left trail (Stewart Canyon) and continue up the canyon. The trail gets fairly close to the edge of the canyon and may feel a little exposed when there's snow. Expect the trail to be broken, but if it isn't you may have to route-find your way up. As long as you are relatively close to the canyon, finding the way up shouldn't be too difficult.

The trail ends after it descends and then crosses a creek that comes down from the right. At the "Poorly Defined Trail Ahead" sign it is best to make your way over to the creek to check out the scenery and then return the way you came in. It is definitely possible to continue up the valley if you still have some energy. There is no real objective or specific destination. Just keep going the same way up the valley until you've had enough and then turn around.

29 Taylor Lake

A long grind up to a picturesque lake. The actual snowshoeing is at an intermediate level, but the sheer length of this trip and significant elevation gain required push it into the advanced category. The trail is heavily used throughout the year, so trail-breaking may not be a concern. Microspikes or just hiking boots can usually get you most of the way, but as usual it is recommended that snowshoes are worn in order to minimize damage to the trail.

DIFFICULTY: advanced
LAKE HEIGHT: 2078 m
ELEVATION GAIN: 585 m
ROUND-TRIP DISTANCE: 13 km
ROUND-TRIP TIME: 4–6 hours
MAPS: 82 N/08 Lake Louise, Gem Trek Lake Louise and Yoho

Directions

Driving west on Highway 1, turn left into the Taylor parking lot, about 7.6 km west of the Highway 93 turnoff. The trail is very obvious almost all of the way up, so a detailed route description is not required. If you end up trail-breaking through deep powder in thick forest, you are desperately off route!

Go through the gate, turn right and snowshoe for about 200 m to a trail sign. Turn left and away you go. Taylor Creek is soon crossed on a bridge and then the trail starts gaining elevation. Hopefully, you brought a few friends to chat with along the way. It feels like a million kilometres to the next bridge!

Shortly after crossing a subsidiary creek

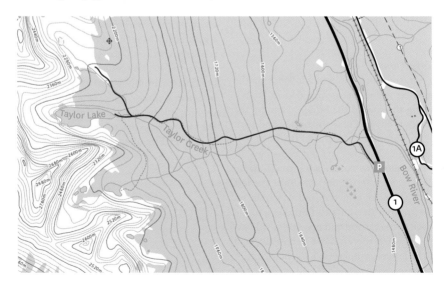

Taylor Lake, with Mount Bell (left) and Panorama Ridge (right).

on another bridge, the trail forks at an unsigned and easily missed intersection (GR638834, 2074 m) – look for flagging in the trees. Straight (right) goes to Panorama Meadows and left goes to Taylor Lake. Turn left and follow the trail and a sign to the lake outlet at GR636833.

The lake is backdropped by the impressively steep walls of Mount Bell and the less steep but still cool slopes of Panorama Ridge. Snowshoeing around or across the lake doesn't provide significantly better views – best to just hangout at the outlet and enjoy the surroundings.

If you are looking for more exercise or different scenery, consider extending the day to Panorama Meadows. Otherwise, return the same way. Even though the descent is mercifully easy when compared with the ascent, it still feels like a million kilometres!

Panorama Meadows

This extension of the Taylor Lake trip gets you to an open meadow on the southeast side of convoluted Panorama Ridge. It adds 3 km return of horizontal distance and 100 m of vertical gain to an already lengthy day. On a clear day you will get an excellent view of the steep east face of Panorama Ridge. The view from the meadow is pleasant but hardly sensational! Good for the exercise.

Directions
Return to the intersection at GR638834 and turn left (northwest), paralleling the subsidiary creek. The trail may vary from year to year, depending on snow conditions, but in general follows the creek on its left side, goes through the trees near the creek and then traverses right into the creek, before reaching the meadow. Around GR633838, leave the creek, cutting to the left and then resume travel northwest into the meadow.

The meadow is a great place to see Panorama Ridge's formidable east side. (SOISTHEMAN)

For beginners, this is the end of the line (GR632838, 2168 m). Advanced snowshoers can ascend "Panorama Hill" at the right side of the valley (see *Snowshoeing in the Canadian Rockies, 2nd Edition*). Enjoy the great view of Panorama Ridge and then return the same way.

30 Ink Pots

This is a great trip that takes you into the beautiful Johnston Creek valley. Travel is easy throughout, but the 420 m of elevation gain make this an intermediate route, perhaps even an advanced route for those snowshoers not used to large elevation gains. The trip can be completed as a loop route with the very popular Johnston Canyon. Choose a clear day to best enjoy the wonderful scenery at the Ink Pots.

DIFFICULTY: intermediate

TOTAL ELEVATION GAIN: 420 m

ROUND-TRIP DISTANCE: 12–14 km

ROUND-TRIP TIME: 3–5 hours

MAPS: 82 O/05 Castle Mountain, 82 O/04 Banff, Gem Trek Banff

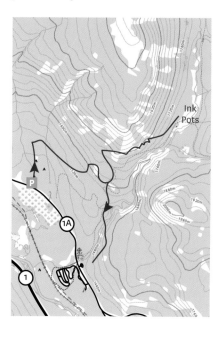

Directions

The trailhead (Moose Meadows hiking trail, not Moose Meadows Exhibition) sits about 4.6 km east of Castle Junction, or 2 km west of the Johnston Canyon parking lot on the north side of Highway 1A.

From the trailhead kiosk, a trail sign is immediately visible, directing you to follow the trail up and to the right. The next 3.2 km take you through light forest. Trail signs are sporadic, but the path should be fairly obvious. More than likely the trail will already be broken, and it will be just a matter of following those who have gone before. Also, this trail can be popular with skiers. The wide path has plenty of space for separate tracks, so try to stay off any ski tracks that have been made.

At the important junction, 3.2 km up, turn left. The trail gains elevation on the far east shoulder of Helena Ridge before plummeting down into the valley to the north. You'll lose about 90 m of elevation on the way down to the Ink Pots. The scenery finally starts to open up as you approach

the Ink Pots, the aesthetic form of Mount Ishbel dominating the view.

The Ink Pots themselves may be a little disappointing in winter, as their greenish-blue hues are not as vibrant. Of course, some or all of the seven or eight pools may be completely covered by snow and ice. However, the pristine valley around them should more than make up for the "shortcomings" of the wintery pots. Although the only visible named peaks are Mount Ishbel

The Ink Pots and Mount Ishbel make a great combination. (Shawn Benbow)

and Block Mountain, the valley is home to many striking outliers and ridges.

The "Stay On the Designated Trail" signs are primarily geared toward summer visitors, but this environmentally sensitive area deserves the same consideration even when snow protects (to a degree) the vegetation. If you decide to venture farther north for some extra exercise, stay on Johnston Creek Trail. The trail crosses the creek on a bridge and then heads north. There really isn't too much point going any farther unless you plan to winter camp at the campground, 1.7 km north. It's probably better to hang out around the Ink Pots and take in the scenery.

For the return trip, grind your way back up the shoulder of Helena Ridge (another 90 m of elevation gain) and then descend to the aforementioned junction. Here you have two options. Easiest and fastest is to return the way you came in via Moose Meadows Trail. The longer but more interesting route is via Johnston Canyon. Be warned, however, that you will be sharing this trail with a multitude of hikers, thereby preventing a Mach 2 descent! Keep your snowshoes on for this route, as the trail gets very icy. Once back to Highway 1A, a 2-km hike along the road takes you back to Moose Meadows.

Highway 93 South

Highway 93 South is the gateway to British Columbia's Kootenay National Park. There are only a handful of easy snowshoe routes along the north end of Highway 93 South, but those that are available to the beginner shoer are terrific! Marble Canyon is hands down the most scenic and interesting trip in the entire book that is under one hour in duration.

The park receives significant amounts of snow throughout the season and once it falls, it stays. However, relatively low starting elevations for the trips described here mean that the snow on the routes will be the first to melt. January, February and early March are usually the best months to visit the area.

Of special interest along and around the north section of the highway are the scars of a major forest fire that ripped through the park in 2003. Though innumerable dead and blackened trees still stand, the new growth is now emerging in green splendour. Of course snow hides most of the new trees in winter. Best to visit the park in summer if you want to see them.

Vermilion Peak makes a great backdrop for Marble Canyon.

31 Boom Lake

If the huge elevation gain required for Taylor Lake (page 130)doesn't appeal to you, there's Boom Lake – similar terrific view with less than a third of the uphill grind. Do the trip in the morning or early afternoon to increase the chances of the sun illuminating the beautiful view at the lake. The trail is popular with skiers. Stay well to the right side of the trail to avoid collisions.

DIFFICULTY: intermediate
LAKE HEIGHT: 1893 m
ELEVATION GAIN: 175 m
ROUND-TRIP DISTANCE: 10.8 km
ROUND-TRIP TIME: 2.5–4.5 hours
MAPS: 82 N/08 Lake Louise,
   Gem Trek Kootenay National Park

Directions

Drive 7 km south on Highway 93 and turn right, into the Boom Lake parking lot. Instructions are hardly required, as the trail is obvious throughout. Also, Boom Lake Trail is one of those rare trails that is easily wide enough to support a snowshoe track and one or two ski tracks. Snowshoe on the far right side of the trail and use the same track on the return trip. This will allow skiers to

Bad timing! The sun had already set over the mountains by the time I reached the lake. Go late in the season and early in the day for a much better view.

create an uptrack in the centre and a down-track on the left or vice versa.

The trail crosses Boom Creek right away, goes a short distance and eventually switch-backs to the left. A steady but gentle elevation gain ensues. At the 2.3-km mark a trail sign is reached. Right goes to O'Brien Lake. Go straight. The next 3.1 km are more undulating but still very easy and obvious. Near the end, the trail descends down and to the left to the lake. It drops you out at the lakeshore (GR639795), about 600 m west of the lake outlet.

When the sun is shining on the lake and surrounding mountains you are in for a treat. Boom Mountain, outliers of Chimney Peak, Quadra Mountain and Bident Mountain all tower majestically over the lake. You can snowshoe in either direction along the lake, but there are some avalanche slopes coming down off Mount Bell to the north. Stay away from those ones. If the lake is frozen, going over to the south side will grant you better views of Bell and Bident. Return the same way.

32 Stanley Glacier Valley

This valley is famous for world-class ice climbs (Nemesis and French Reality) and also the receding Stanley Glacier. Unfortunately, the upper valley is prone to avalanches and therefore off limits to those without avalanche training and gear. However, the beginner snowshoer can go far enough into the valley to get a good workout and some great views. The sun doesn't get into this valley much, so late-season, late-day trips are recommended.

DIFFICULTY: advanced
MAXIMUM HEIGHT: 1800 m
ELEVATION GAIN: 200 m
ROUND-TRIP DISTANCE: 4.6 km
ROUND-TRIP TIME: 1.5–3 hours
MAPS: 82 N/1 Mount Goodsir,
Gem Trek Kootenay National Park

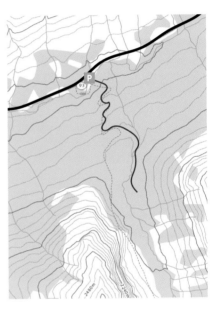

Directions

Drive 13 km south on Highway 93 and turn left, into the Stanley Glacier parking lot. Snowshoe down to the Vermilion River and cross it on a bridge. The trail now takes a series of switchbacks through an area of burnt forest, up to the valley above. When it levels off you are treated to a great view of the valley ahead, as well as all the mountains to the west, south and north. Mount Whymper is especially eye-catching.

Start going up the valley. The trail soon curves to the left and goes down a little before crossing Stanley Creek on a log bridge. You can continue up the valley for another 200 m or so before getting into avalanche terrain. Unfortunately, trees hide much of the view here, but going farther may put you at risk. Turn around and return the same way. If this trip wasn't enough for the day, check out the Paint Pots, Marble Canyon and/or Boom Lake.

ABOVE: *The view into the Stanley Glacier Valley.*

LEFT: *Even in the trees, the scenery can be breathtaking. (SOISTHEMAN)*

33 Marble Canyon

Marble Canyon is awesome! It's short, easy and throughout has fantastic views of the canyon and surrounding mountains. There are a couple of steeper sections that are perfect for snowshoes. I witnessed several people on foot struggling up the first slope. If the trip is too short, you can extend the day by snowshoeing on a good trail down to the Paint Pots (page 143) or take a little stroll up Tokumm Valley.

DIFFICULTY: easy

ELEVATION GAIN: 50 m

ROUND-TRIP DISTANCE: 1.6 km

ROUND-TRIP TIME: 0.5–1 hours

MAPS: 82 N/1 Mount Goodsir,
Gem Trek Kootenay National Park

Directions

Drive 17 km south on Highway 93 and turn right, into the Marble Canyon parking lot. Two trails leave the parking lot: one for Marble Canyon and the other for Tokumm Valley. Take the Marble Canyon trail that lies to the left. No route instructions are

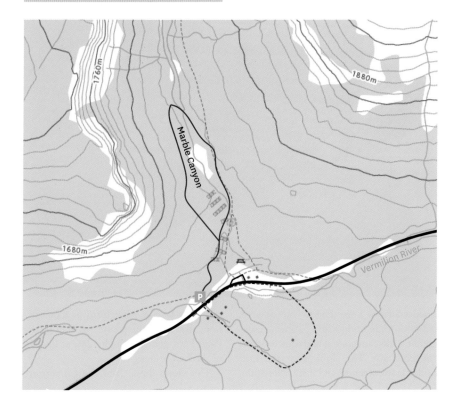

ABOVE: *Winter splendour in Marble Canyon.*

BELOW: *Great views of the Vermilion River and Stanley Peak along the shoreline.*

required from here. Follow the obvious path. Multiple bridges and pathways cross and line the canyon and each one is worth checking out. The slope after the first bridge is the steepest and if icy will require snowshoes or another form of foot traction. Also note the connector trail to the Paint Pots, going through a gate at the end of the first bridge.

The views down into the canyon are

amazing. However, also be aware that as the snow piles up on the bridges, the rails get lower and lower, relatively speaking. At times, it might be easy to fall over a railing on one of the bridges. I would keep kids away from the edges.

Once you get to the end, either return the same way, or for some extra exercise go north to find the Tokumm Valley trail. Then follow it in a northwesterly direction until you've had enough.

A better way to extend your day is by descending down to the Paint Pots trail, although the trip from the Paint Pots to Marble Canyon and then back down again may be preferable.

Paint Pots Connector

Note that there is a warning from Parks Canada about danger from falling trees on this trail. The burnt trees from the 2003 forest fire are susceptible to fall without warning. Be aware of this if you are going to use this trail.

The trail starts right after the first bridge. It curves up and around the canyon below and then starts gently downhill, eventually paralleling the Vermilion River, but high above it. When the trail gets close to the river, you can either stay on the trail or, if the adventurer in you is awake, go right down to the river and follow it downstream. Depending on the snow and ice conditions along the river, this route may require route-finding around deadfall and some trickier terrain. However, the scenic rewards are well worth it. The trail is never too far away if you decide to get back on it.

The connector trail is 2.7 km in length. If you did take the scenic route, you'll want to return to the trail about 500 m before the end. Eventually you'll end up at the bridge that crosses the Vermilion River and then goes to the Paint Pots parking lot. Either check out the Paint Pots area or return the way you came. Hiking back up to the Marble Canyon parking lot using the highway is not recommended because of the potentially high volume of fast-moving traffic.

Lake Louise

If you have never heard of Lake Louise, you are either new to this province or new to this planet! To call the lake "the jewel of the Canadian Rockies" is certainly an accurate description. The unequalled appearance of Lake Louise in calendars, books, magazines and on postcards is but a small testament to the power this body of water (or ice, in this case) holds over the viewer. I cannot begin to count how many times I've been to the lake over the years, and I still get that "deer in the headlights" look every time I see it!

A national park pass is required for all trips in the Lake Louise area.

The classic lakeshore view toward Mount Victoria and Victoria Glacier. Note the skating rink if you want to bring your skates.

34 Lake Louise and Shoreline

Don't expect to be alone on this route! The obvious trail goes west, around the north side of the lake. Of course, if the lake is sufficiently frozen, it is also possible to snowshoe directly across it as you head toward its west end. Backdropped by magnificent Mount Victoria and its glacier, the scenery and views are impressive throughout.

DIFFICULTY: easy	
ELEVATION GAIN: minimal	
ROUND-TRIP DISTANCE: 4 km	
ROUND-TRIP TIME: 1–2 hours	
MAPS: 82 N/08 Lake Louise, Gem Trek Lake Louise and Yoho	

Directions

Drive to Lake Louise and take the 4-km road to the chateau. The east end of the lake is only a few hundred metres from the public parking lot. Pick either shoreline to follow (the north being more popular and well packed down), or snowshoe directly across. While the terrific view of Mount Victoria is

Looking down the lake, with Mount Lefroy becoming more prominent at the left. Photo taken from just above the shoreline trail.

ever present, the equally impressive Mount Lefroy soon makes an appearance.

At the west end of the lake sits a world-famous climbing area, appropriately named "Back of the Lake." Also be sure to check out the 110-m ice climb, Louise Falls, before returning to the chateau via the lake surface or the shoreline. For the most variety it might make sense to return via the route you didn't use on the way in (again, as long as the lake is frozen solid).

35 Mirror Lake and Lake Agnes

Although it's a fair climb to reach Mirror Lake, the gentle grade makes travel quite easy. The scenery is respectable, but continuing on to Lake Agnes rewards you with spectacular views of the lake and surrounding mountains. Unfortunately, you must travel through a short section of avalanche terrain to get to Agnes. Avalanches that run over the trail are rare, but it's best to check with the park wardens before you go. You'll want to pick a clear day and go in the morning to get the best sun on the lakes.

DIFFICULTY: intermediate to Mirror Lake; advanced to Lake Agnes

ELEVATION GAIN: 295 m to Mirror Lake; add 90 m to Lake Agnes

ROUND-TRIP DISTANCE: 5.4 km return for Mirror Lake; add 1.8 km return for Lake Agnes

ROUND-TRIP TIME: 2.5–4 hours

MAPS: 82 N/08 Lake Louise, Gem Trek Lake Louise and Yoho

Directions

Drive to Lake Louise and take the 4-km road to the chateau. From the public parking lot, find your way to the shore and start snowshoeing (or hiking) along the upper trail around the right (north) side of the lake. The signed trailhead is a short distance up. Make sure you are on the Lake Agnes snowshoe/hiking trail and not on one of the telemarking trails.

The trail is usually well packed down,

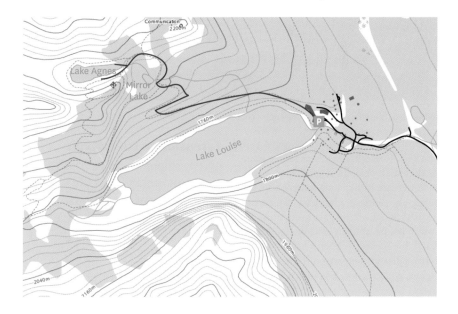

Mirror Lake, with the Big Beehive towering above it.

so wearing snowshoes will improve your traction. Route-finding is never an issue, as the trail is obvious. It ascends the steep, forested face in two long switchbacks at a relatively gentle grade. After the second switchback, the route goes deeper into the forest before spitting you out at Mirror Lake. The scenery at Mirror Lake is decent, but it pales in comparison to that at Lake Agnes, which is now less than a kilometre away.

Extension to Lake Agnes

Again, there is some avalanche potential going to Lake Agnes. The trail is never steep, but if the slopes above the trail slide, the trail (with you on it!) may get buried. Remember to check in with park wardens before taking this trip extension.

ABOVE: *Lake Agnes. The striking peak at the left is called Devil's Thumb. Mount Whyte sits at the centre, and Mount Niblock is the small but obvious block at the far right. Whyte and Niblock are terrific summer scrambles, described in Alan Kane's* Scrambles in the Canadian Rockies.

BELOW: *The summit block of Mount Niblock, as seen from a short distance along the south shore of Lake Agnes.*

Directions

Continue north up the trail and then swing around to the west for the final push to the lake and teahouse. Hurry through this section and advance one person at a time, just in case. The only snowshoeing challenge might come right at the end when you have to ascend the snow-covered stairs. Be careful here. A slip could be very painful.

Unfortunately, a hot cup of tea will not be waiting for you at the famous Lake Agnes Teahouse. The teahouse closes for the winter. However, what may be waiting (weather permitting) is a stunning view of the snow-covered lake, backdropped by the wonderful forms of Mounts Niblock and Whyte and the strikingly jagged rock formations of Devil's Thumb. Hopefully, all will be bathed in beautiful sunlight.

Sitting at an elevation of 2134 m, the lake remains frozen through most of the winter. Snowshoeing across it is generally quite safe. Otherwise, snowshoe around the perimeter on either side to see more of the beautiful surroundings. Do not venture too far along the side of the lake. Although unlikely, avalanches from the slopes above are possible.

Also, though the temptation may be great, avoid attempting the trail to the Big Beehive, 185 m above. This could put you on serious avalanche terrain. On return, the same is true for the traverse to the Little Beehive. Unless you are experienced on steep terrain and can assess avalanche conditions, stay clear of these detours.

Return the same way you came up. Wearing snowshoes for the descent will enable you to fly down the trail in no time.

Yoho

Yoho National Park lies on the eastern edge of British Columbia and starts about 10 km west of Lake Louise, on the Trans-Canada Highway. The park is the smallest in area of the four contiguous national parks (Banff, Kootenay and Jasper completing the list) but still has great potential for good snowshoeing routes. Sherbrooke Lake and Emerald Lake, both in Yoho, are two of the more scenic trips in the Rockies.

Due to the park's proximity to the Continental Divide, the eastern side of Yoho receives enormous volumes of snow throughout the winter and is a good destination when areas on the east side of the Rockies are melting out. However, the southwest section of the park is approximately 400 m below the eastern side. The snow in the

Awesome weather and scenery at Emerald Lake.

southwest will melt much earlier than that in the east. Keep this in mind for Wapta Falls (page 159).

A national park pass is required for all trips in Yoho.

36 Sherbrooke Lake

This is yet another "wait for a clear day" snowshoe trip. The views at the south end of this huge lake are fantastic. Snowshoes with good crampons are a must for the relentless grade and sometimes icy nature of the trail. This trail is frequently used by skiers as a descent route from Waputik Icefield. Be aware that they may be coming down the trail at significant speed, and get out of their way if that happens.

DIFFICULTY: advanced

ELEVATION GAIN: approximately 200 m

ROUND-TRIP DISTANCE: 6.2 km

ROUND-TRIP TIME: 2.5–3.5 hours

MAPS: 82 N/08 Lake Louise,
Gem Trek Lake Louise and Yoho

Directions

Drive west on the Trans-Canada Highway, past Lake Louise toward Field. Continue about 1.8 km past the Lake O'Hara turnoff and turn right at the Great Divide Lodge. The trailhead is at the northwest end of the parking lot.

Put on your snowshoes and get ready for a solid 200 m of elevation gain in about 1.4 horizontal kilometres. The grade is never

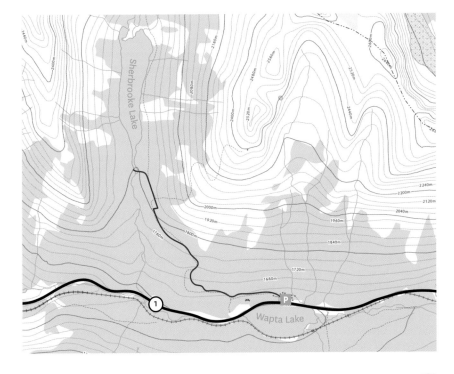

Who knew the Karate Kid would be hanging out at Sherbrooke Lake? And he's wearing snowshoes! Mounts Niles and Daly rise behind the lake.

obscenely steep, but it is quite relentless and should elevate your heart rate. The trail basically takes a long sweeping line along and up the southwest side of Paget Peak. Depending on who broke the trail, it may or may not follow the summer trail for the first 1.4 km. If the trail hasn't been broken (very unlikely), route-finding could be a challenge, so you may want to bail and try Ross Lake instead.

Most of the elevation is gained in the first 1.4 km, at which point you will hopefully arrive at a sign for Sherbrooke Lake and Paget Lookout. Take the left fork to Sherbrooke Lake. Travel north on more level terrain for 1.6 km to the south end of the lake. Again, the specific location of the trail may differ from year to year and with it the amount of extra elevation gain. Expect at least one more section of strenuous uphill travel and then a gentle descent to the lake.

If you have heeded my advice about waiting for a clear day, and the weather has cooperated, the scenery at the lake should not disappoint in the least. The massive and impressively steep peak towering over the west side of the lake is Mount Ogden,

with the less impressive Paget Peak on the east side. The very distinctive and shapely peak at the north end is Mount Niles, and Mount Daly sits to the right of Niles; both are scrambles described in Alan Kane's *Scrambles in the Canadian Rockies*. Note the little pyramid between Niles and Daly. And if that wasn't enough, turn around and you are treated to wonderful views of Mount Victoria and Cathedral Mountain.

Explore the south end of the lake as conditions allow. At certain times of the year, when some but not all of the snow has melted, the snow scenery can be spectacular. Crossing the outlet of the lake also allows you to see more of the terrific views, but do so with care.

The south end of the lake is the end of the line for beginner snowshoers. Going farther puts you into avalanche terrain. Although it is highly unlikely that an avalanche could reach you if you were to snowshoe north up the middle of the lake, on the day I was there small avalanches on both sides of the lake could be heard at unnervingly regular intervals. Return the same way you came in.

ABOVE: *To the south lie the familiar forms of Victoria, Huber and Cathedral.*

BELOW: *The steep east face and corniced ridge of Mount Ogden. When the cornices collapse, they can trigger huge avalanches down the face.*

37 Emerald Lake

Missing the beautiful bright-green waters of Emerald Lake by snow-shoeing around or across it in winter is a small price to pay for the fantastic scenery around this pristine lake. Waiting for a clear day is a must here – you will be disappointed otherwise. If you are unsure of the safety of the lake ice, ask the staff at the lodge. Otherwise, use the summer trail. The ice should be sufficiently strong for your purposes during January, February and March.

DIFFICULTY: easy

ELEVATION GAIN: minimal

ROUND-TRIP DISTANCE: 5.3 km

ROUND-TRIP TIME: 1.5–2.5 hours

MAPS: 82 N/07 Golden,
Gem Trek Lake Louise and Yoho

Directions

Drive to Field, BC, on the Trans-Canada Highway and turn right (north) onto Emerald Lake Road, a few kilometres west of Field. It's about 9.2 km to the Emerald Lake parking lot (don't park in the overnight guest parking).

Hike or snowshoe down to the lake. The direction of travel may depend on the time of day. Very early morning trips favour a clockwise direction because of the sun's position in the sky. Mid-morning and later are better done counter-clockwise. Counter-clockwise is described below.

Although there is a summer hiking trail around the entire lake, the winter snow-shoe/ski route usually stays right on the lake, near the shore and sometimes well away from it. Be aware that the ski and

The awe-inspiring peaks of the President Range are a constant companion throughout the trip.

Some poor soul learning that wearing snowshoes does not guarantee good balance!

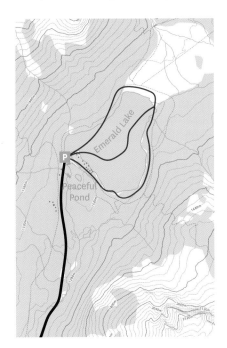

snowshoe routes can be one and the same. There is tons of space for everyone, so, as usual, stay off any ski tracks. For early-season trips and when the ice on the lake is unstable, find the summer hiking route. Travelling this route may require a very healthy dose of trail-breaking.

From beginning to end the surrounding views are magnificent. Although you are staring at the same mountains throughout, the different angles and new scenery appearing now and then should be plenty to keep you entertained. Starting from the southeast and going counter-clockwise, you will be enjoying the striking forms of Mount Burgess, Wapta Mountain, Michael Peak, the magnificently glaciated President and Vice President and Emerald Peak, looming ominously over the northwest end of the lake.

Even if the scenery from the east side of the lake does start to get monotonous, working your way around to the

Terrific snow scenery at the north end of Emerald Lake.

northeast end is definitely worth the effort. Depending on your specific route, you will eventually run into a wide stretch of braided streams feeding the lake. Trying to negotiate these waterways can be very dangerous. It's best to avoid them by either going around them to the south, travelling directly on the lake, or working your way north to the obvious bridge. The bridge is highly recommended, as it is safe and scenic.

Once over the bridge, continue working your way around the lake. The snow scenery at this end can be very interesting because of snow cover on the undulating terrain. As you start back toward the southwest end of the lake, stay near the shoreline for the first half, but soon you'll want to start moving away from the shore. This is because you are nearing the domain of the infamous Emerald Slide Path. Although perhaps the most innocuous-looking of the mountains around the lake, Emerald Peak is anything

but. The avalanche path on the southeast face of the peak is so well known that it actually gets its own name! Clearly visible, this enormous path collects huge amounts of snow and it slides regularly, often with devastating results. Skiers often "skin up" the path to enjoy an exhilarating and speedy ride down, but only when the avalanche risk is very low. Staying away from the runout zone of the slide path is imperative and that is why the ski and snowshoe trail will veer left, across the lake and toward the lodge. Use that path to enjoy an easy and scenic return to the start.

38 Wapta Falls

Wapta Falls occurs on one of Canada's best-known whitewater rafting waterways – the Kicking Horse River. Getting there can be a somewhat tedious affair, but the falls themselves are spectacular. They are located near the west end of Yoho National Park, about 2.5–3 hours of driving time from Calgary. Make the trip worthwhile: consider waiting for a clear day and completing the Emerald Lake Loop before or after the Wapta Falls trip.

DIFFICULTY: intermediate to advanced
ELEVATION GAIN: approximately 200 m
ROUND-TRIP DISTANCE: 8.6 km
ROUND-TRIP TIME: 2.5–3.5 hours
MAPS: 82 N/02 McMurdo

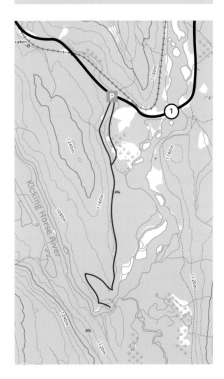

Directions

On the Trans-Canada Highway heading west, drive 24.2 km past Field, BC, to the trailhead on the south side of the road. There is a trailhead sign when approaching from the west, but a sign is mysteriously missing (as of March 2012) when approaching from the east (Field). Be careful not to miss the turnoff. It's 900 m south of the Chancellor Peak Campground turnoff.

Don't be misled at the trailhead kiosk when you read the elevation loss to be 30 m. This is the net loss to the falls only and does not reflect the ups and downs, some of them significant, of the whole trip. Expect about 200 m of total elevation gain and a little more loss.

Snowshoe the gravel road for 2 km to the summer trailhead sign indicating it's another 2.4 km to the falls. Continue going south, following the more or less straight path through the trees. This path is often used by skiers. It is narrow, but with care snowshoers can walk on either side of the path, avoiding any ski tracks. There are short sections where you will have no choice but to walk in the centre.

About 1 km along, the trail gets into thicker forest and descends a little. It then follows a relatively gentle but long ascent on the side of a hill. This takes you to the high point of an embankment, high above the falls. Be sure to take a look down. A metal fence prevents a fatal slip. This section of the trail can be very icy. You may be very thankful for the traction-improving crampons on your snowshoes.

Take in this interesting perspective before you complete the trip down to the base of the falls. The descent is made in two long switchbacks. The first moves well away from the Kicking Horse River, and then a hairpin turn leads backs to the river. You will emerge from the trees and immediately see the falls to your left. From afar they may not look that impressive, but hopefully a closer look will reveal some stunning water/snow/ice scenery.

Before you run over there and inadvertently plunge to an unexpected and icy death, note the following:

1. Between you and the falls are several large pools of water. More than likely they will be frozen and snow-covered, so you can walk right across them. However, if this is not the case, stick to the left, alongside the cliff face.

ABOVE: Looking down on the falls and the extraordinary colours. A large group decide to take in the exquisite beauty of the area. (Shawn Benbow)

BELOW: Jennifer Benbow at the falls. It doesn't get any better than this! (Shawn Benbow)

ABOVE: *Beautiful but very dangerous conditions near the falls. BE CAREFUL!*

BELOW: *Mount Vaux, as seen from the alternative return route by the stream.*

2. A large hill of rock sits in front of the falls. It is steep on the side not facing the falls and even steeper on the other side. Snow and water work together to form interesting formations of ice near the falls. In fact, a significant snow/icebridge was created from the hill to the falls when I visited the area in March of 2012. As beauteous and incredible as these features are, they can also be unstable and extremely dangerous. Explore the area with caution and don't go anywhere that might seem risky.

When you have finished admiring nature's awesome creation, return the same way you came in.

Alternative Return Route

For a little variation and some pleasant scenery on the return trip, once you get back to the summer trailhead, snowshoe about 500 m farther (northwest) and then cut right (northeast) into the forest, quickly arriving in an open area with a stream (perhaps snow-covered). Continue north alongside the stream, enjoying excellent views of Chancellor Peak and statuesque Mount Vaux farther north. You can snowshoe all the way to the road and then back to your vehicle, or cut back to the west when you are close to the road.

Highway 93 North

Highway 93 North, also called the Icefields Parkway, is as breathtaking an area as you can find on this planet – especially when snow has covered the landscape. The highway weaves its way between innumerable, strikingly beautiful peaks and several expansive icefields, the most notable of which is the world-famous Columbia Icefield. Near the south end of the road sits the Wapta Icefield. This sheet of ice and the peaks around it are very accessible to skiers and intermediate to advanced snowshoers.

While routes for the beginner snowshoer along the highway are limited because of access issues and avalanche danger, there are at least six terrific objectives, three of which are described here (see A Beginner's Guide to Snowshoeing in the Canadian Rockies for the other trips).

As well, because of their limited time requirements, it is possible to do multiple routes in one day. Personally, I would wait for a bluebird day and then complete two or three of the routes in the same day. You will experience some of the best and varied scenery in the Rockies, with minimal effort.

Note that this highway is minimally maintained during the winter and can get very icy. Have backup plans just in case. Anything in Lake Louise or Yoho is always a good choice.

Crowfoot Mountain is the backdrop to Bow Lake. Obviously, the bridge sees limited traffic in winter!

39 Bow Lake

As soon as a clear day dawns, you should make your way to Bow Lake. The area around the lake is absolutely magnificent and should be experienced when the skies are clear and the sun is shining. You can explore the area around the colourful Num-Ti-Jah Lodge, snowshoe north along the flanks of "Mount Jimmy Junior" or cross the lake and head toward Bow Falls (or do all three!). This is a must-see area for all outdoor enthusiasts.

Family snowshoeing on Bow Lake. Rogan Nugara leads the way.

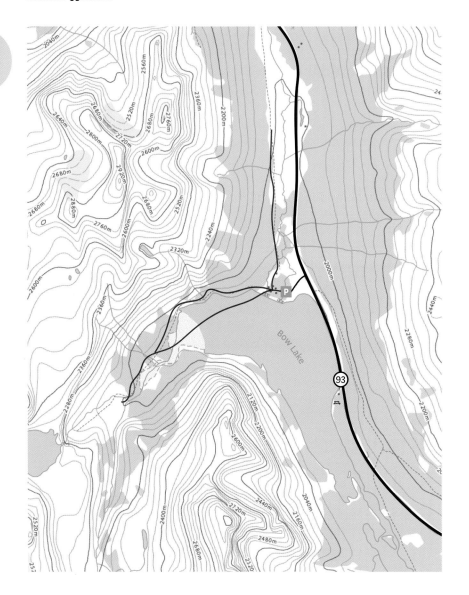

DIFFICULTY: easy

ELEVATION GAIN: 0–80 m maximum

ROUND-TRIP DISTANCE: variable to 8 km maximum

ROUND-TRIP TIME: variable

MAPS: 82 N/09 Hector Lake, Gem Trek Bow Lake and Saskatchewan Crossing

Directions

Drive approximately 36 km north on Highway 93 and turn left into the Num-Ti-Jah Lodge parking lot. Once there, you have a number of options.

Explore

Depending on snow conditions, the area around the lodge can provide many visual rewards. Windblown snow formations, a couple of bridges sticking out of the snow, the historic lodge itself and a creek are but a few of the interesting features. Of course, this is all surrounded by the breathtaking forms of mountains around Bow Lake and on the spectacular Wapta Icefield. Loosely following the northern perimeter of the lake is a great way to see more of the icefield. However, do not go too far beyond the northwest corner of the lake. Avalanche terrain will soon appear to your right if you do push on.

Go North

Snowshoe west past the lodge and turn north. There is a trail here, though it may be impossible to find under all the snow. Go as far as you want in a NNW direction, through light forest and then out into the more open areas, east of the lower slopes of unofficially named "Mount Jimmy Junior." Do not venture west into the vicinity of those slopes, because they can be very avalanche prone. Stay within a few hundred metres of the

At least the bridge can serve as a good spot for a photo! Mark, Keri and the kids, with Observation Peak behind.

Scenery on the north shore of the lake near the parking lot. Portal Peak (centre) and Mount Thompson are but two of the many impressive peaks around the lake.

road. When satiated, either return the way you came in or snowshoe to the road and hike back to the parking area.

Go Across

Crossing the north end of the lake is generally a safe and easy affair. The route is extremely popular with ski and snowshoe mountaineers, so several well-packed trails will invariably go in that direction. Obviously, you'll want to pick the snowshoe trail or make your own if one doesn't exist. Arriving at the gravel flats at the west end of the lake, you can continue on alongside the stream for about 500 m. Beyond this lies a narrow canyon that must be bypassed on the left side. This terrain can be steep and avalanche prone, and it is not for the novice snowshoer. Stop, enjoy the scenery and then return the same way you came.

40 Peyto Lake Viewpoint

When your starting elevation from the car is close to 2100 m, good to spectacular views are guaranteed within minutes. Such is the case with Peyto Lake Viewpoint. The amazing view of Peyto Lake, far below, is about a 10–15 minute snowshoe from the parking lot. You can then do an extension to the glades south of the viewpoint. As at Bow Lake, if you are in the area and enjoying good weather, this is a must-do trip.

DIFFICULTY: easy

ELEVATION GAIN: 25–50 m

ROUND-TRIP DISTANCE: 1.2–2 km

ROUND-TRIP TIME: 0.5–2 hours

MAPS: 82 N/09 Hector Lake, 82 N/10 Blaeberry River, Gem Trek Bow Lake and Saskatchewan Crossing

Directions

Drive approximately 40 km north on Highway 93 and turn left into the Bow Summit /Peyto Lake parking lot. Follow the road to the parking area, which can be very busy, especially on weekends. This area is deservedly popular with skiers wanting to get in some turns, and it is sometimes the

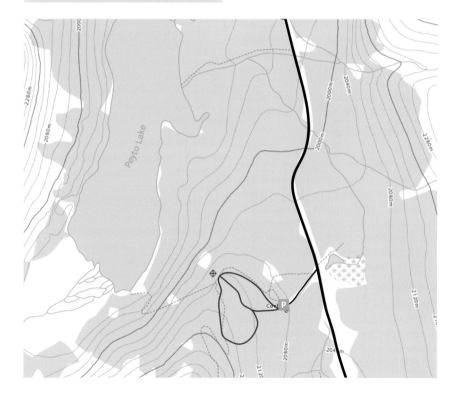

The classic view from Peyto Lake Viewpoint.

location for mountaineering courses such as AST 1 or 2.

There are two loops to complete. The direction of travel may depend on whether a trail has been broken or not. I recommend using the summer interpretive trail to go directly to the viewpoint and then head south to complete the other loop. There is a series of interpretive plaques mounted on blue supports along here that you could follow, but the plaques are far between, the second is not visible from the first and so forth. Therefore, if no previous track exists, finding these signs may require some searching. If this is the case, it may be better to do the route in a clockwise direction.

Counter-Clockwise

Go to the north end of the parking lot and look for a trail. If there isn't one, make your own, heading northwest and then west. Try to follow the interpretive signs as much as possible. The viewpoint is about 600 m from the parking lot. If at any time you get lost or disoriented, turn around and follow your tracks back to the parking lot, then use the clockwise route.

Clockwise

The trail starts by the kiosk, arriving quickly at the unplowed road. The road goes up and to the right for a while before swinging around to the left (south). A sign pointing at lofty Observation Peak (a terrific scramble

in the summer) is quickly reached. At the sign, cut back to the right (northwest) and go slightly downhill to the viewpoint, about 100 m away.

The Viewpoint

As expected, the highlight of the panorama is the distinctive outline of Peyto Lake, nestled under Caldron Peak's impressive east face. To the southwest lies the tongue of Peyto Glacier, one of several gateways to Wapta Icefield. Peyto Peak lies to the left of Caldron. The striking peak due south of the viewpoint is an outlier of "Mount Jimmy Simpson." A close look may reveal multiple paths of S turns made by skiers enjoying the terrain.

Second Loop

From the viewpoint, snowshoe southeast back to the Observation Peak sign, about 100 m away. Continue going south through open terrain. Again, there may be tracks to follow or you may be forging your own path. There are two important things to remember here: don't snowshoe on ski tracks and don't follow them southwest toward the steeper and more dangerous slopes of the Jimmy Simpson outlier. Instead, stay south on gentle terrain, eventually making a counter-clockwise loop back to the unplowed road or to the parking lot.

41 Waterfowl Lakes

You don't even need to get out of your vehicle to be blown away by the view from the east side of Waterfowl Lakes! Snowshoeing alongside the lakeshore on a clear day can be an awe-inspiring and beautifully serene experience at once. The extension to Chephren Lake presents a more challenging objective that is equally stunning.

DIFFICULTY: easy for Waterfowl Lakes; advanced to Chephren Lake

ELEVATION GAIN: minimal for Waterfowl Lakes; 120 m to Chephren Lake

ROUND-TRIP DISTANCE: 0.5–4 km for Waterfowl Lakes; 3.4–5.4 km for Chephren Lake

ROUND-TRIP TIME: 0.5–3 hours

MAPS: 82 N/15 Mistaya Lake, Gem Trek Bow Lake and Saskatchewan Crossing

Directions

North of Waterfowl Lakes Campground, there are two pullouts for Waterfowl Lakes. The northernmost pullout is recommended as a starting point and is situated 2.2 km north of the Waterfowl Campground's unplowed turnoff (1.3 km north of the first pullout).

The lake is only a couple of minutes from the pullout. Descend to the lakeshore and take in the outstanding views of Mount Chephren and Howse Peak to the west. If

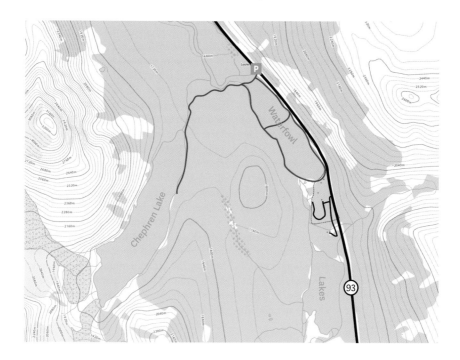

One of the most impressive views the Icefields Parkway has to offer. From left to right, Howse Peak, mighty Mount Chephren, Epaulette Mountain, Kaufmann Peaks and Mount Sarbach.

clouds cover the mountains, you will be very disappointed; if the skies are clear, you will be blown away! There are two fairly extreme climbing routes (Wild Thing and East Face) that go right up the east face of Chephren. When I sprout wings I may try one of them.

Options are numerous at this point:

1. Snowshoe southeast, directly on the lake or on the bank of the lake, for a kilometre or so, and then return the same way. Views toward Epaulette Mountain, Kaufmann Peaks and Mount Sarbach, to the north of Chephren, improve as you go farther south.
2. Snowshoe the entire perimeter of the lake, crossing over the lake at the northwest end on return.
3. Snowshoe southeast for a short distance and then go across the lake to the west side. Any trip across the lake grants you excellent views of Mounts Noyes and Weed to the southeast.
4. Snowshoe northwest, cross the lake and go toward Chephren Lake.
5. For an easy but slightly longer trip, I would recommend snowshoeing the entire perimeter of the lake, or a portion of it. You can always just do half of the lake.

If you are looking to really take advantage of the day, combine the last two options and go all the way to Chephren Lake, as described below.

Chephren Lake

Although unnecessary, first go southeast down the lake for a little while. This exposes you to full views of the lake and surrounding mountains. Next, cross to the west side of the lake, provided the surface is sufficiently frozen. Turn northwest and follow the lakeshore to the wide lake outlet at the northwest end of the lake, very soon to become the Mistaya River.

The river goes west and then dips to the southwest before turning to the northwest. Here you get an open view of the river running northwest. Although there is a creek that joins Chephren Lake to the Mistaya River a short distance downstream, this creek is hard to find and brutally hard to follow. The best route once you get to this open area (GR241446) is to cut left (southwest) into the trees and make your way up and through the trees, eventually intersecting the aforementioned creek. Expect trail-breaking for this entire section to be very gruelling. Once you find the creek, follow it in a southerly direction up to Chephren Lake.

The river dips southwest. Around the corner is where you leave the river to bushwhack to the creek that drains Chephren Lake.

Again, views toward Mount Chephren and Howse Peak are outstanding. You can snowshoe south along the east shoreline (the west is not recommended, because of potential avalanches) for any distance you feel like and then return the same way. The lake is deceivingly long. Snowshoeing all the way to the south side will perhaps be a little too ambitious, although the view of Chephren will be awesome.

Information Centres

When looking for advice and information regarding trail conditions, trip suggestions, weather forecasts, accommodations etc., you can visit or call one of numerous information centres in the Rockies.

Highway 40 South

The Barrier Lake Information Centre is located 8 km south on Highway 40 and is open Monday to Thursday, 9 a.m.–4 p.m., and Friday to Sunday, 9 a.m.–5 p.m. Call 403-673-3985 for inquiries.

Kananaskis Lakes Trail

The Peter Lougheed Visitor Centre is located 3.6 km along Kananaskis Trail and is open year-round. Call 403-591-6322 for inquiries.

Banff

The Banff Information Centre is located at 224 Banff Avenue in the Town of Banff. The centre's hours of operation vary throughout the year. Call 403-762-1550 for inquiries.

Lake Louise

The Lake Louise Visitor Information Centre is located in the Village of Lake Louise, next to Samson Mall. The centre's hours of operation vary throughout the year. Call 403-522-3833 for inquiries.

Yoho

The Yoho National Park Visitor Centre is located at 5764 Trans-Canada Highway, Field, BC. Call 250-343-6783 for inquiries.